I0616157

THE
TEACHER
TAKEOVER

Reclaiming Our Classrooms,
Communities, and Mental Health

DR. ADRIENNE SIMMONS

Some names and identifying characteristics have been changed to protect the privacy of the individuals involved.

Copyright © 2024 by Adrienne Simmons.

All rights reserved. Published by AJS Solutions LLC. No part of this publication may be reproduced, stored in a retrieval system, or transmitted in any form or by any means, electronic, mechanical, photocopying, recording, or otherwise, without written permission of the publisher. Requests for permission should be addressed to AJS Solutions LLC, Tucker, Georgia 30084.

ISBN 979-8-218-56462-9 (Paperback)

ISBN 979-8-218-57825-1 (Ebook)

Library of Congress Control Number: 2024927207

Printed in the U.S.A.

Visit www.TeacherTakeover.com

DEDICATION

This book is dedicated to my first superhero, my mother, Doris Wilburn. My mom would tell you that she and my father raised four highly successful daughters: one a technology specialist, one an obstetrician-gynecologist, one a marketing director, and then me, the education executive. What she would also tell you is that it was *not* easy getting us across the finish line. My father was often away at sea as a sailor in the United States Navy. During his intermittent absences, my mother was prompted to galvanize her network of family and friends to help with the heavy load. She rang the alarm for other superheroes in the community to step up and lend a helping hand.

Mom, thank you for teaching me that superheroes wear dresses, too. Furthermore, I don't take for granted that you demonstrated to me the significance of calling for backup when needed. It is this core value that propelled me to write *The Teacher Takeover*. I hope that my words are transformative and that readers will experience a sense of empowerment in responding to the long-overdue call for action on behalf of one of America's most marginalized professions.

CONTENTS

INTRODUCTION 7

CHAPTER 1: Mass Exodus 13

    Inadequate Pay.. 15

    The Influence of Politics 18

    Lack of Respect for the Teaching Profession 20

    We Need Good Teachers to Stay..23

CHAPTER 2: Define Your Why and Commit to the Heart Work.... 25

    The Teacher Takeover Mindset 27

    Be the Expert 31

    Find Your People 32

CHAPTER 3: Dare to Disrupt the Status Quo............................35

CHAPTER 4: Traditional Leadership.......................................39

    Transformational Leadership..41

    Adaptive Leadership 44

    Applying Adaptive Leadership 48

    The Truth About Leadership 51

    Teacher Takeover Testimonial...53

CHAPTER 5: Advocacy..57

    Advocacy Defined 57

    Advocate-worthy Causes in Education.................................58

    How to Advocate Effectively..70

    Teacher Takeover Testimonial...76

CHAPTER 6: Governance...**79**

What to Expect as a School Board Member 80

The 5P Framework of School Board Governance...................83

Board Member & Superintendent Relationship 90

Board Member & District Staff Relationships....................... 94

Board Member & Constituency or Community Member Relationships.. 96

Board Member & Student Relationships 103

Teacher Takeover Testimonial...106

CHAPTER 7: The Significance of Self-Care and How to Achieve Work-Life Balance **107**

The Power of Sick Days and Employee Assistance Programs..... 109

Get Moving 110

Find Momentum in Mentorship 112

Prioritize Fun 115

Teacher Takeover Testimonial...118

CHAPTER 8: Ready...Set...Act!...**121**

The Teacher Takeover ABCs...123

Teacher Takeover Testimonial...125

CHAPTER 9: Epilogue..**127**

NOTES...**131**

INTRODUCTION

———

I f you are reading this book, you are likely a classroom teacher at a pivotal professional crossroads. You are fed up with your work conditions. Your administrators expect you to come to work early and stay late. The amount of paperwork that you must complete daily is becoming insurmountable. Your weekends seem non-existent because you are busy grading assignments and preparing for next week's instruction. The disrespect that comes from parents, students, politicians, administrators, and even your colleagues is at an all-time high. You are considering leaving the teaching profession...which is something you never dreamed you would do.

I know this feeling firsthand. I was once a classroom teacher.

I taught students in grades K–5 for six years, and I supported teachers as an instructional coach for an additional five years. I remember believing my hard work was too often overlooked by school leaders. I recall the 'Teacher of the Year' award feeling like a popularity contest, with those teachers that were the most extroverted always seeming to win the prize. Of course, as school staff, we were rarely (if ever) presented with academic data or instructional evidence to influence our decision ahead of voting for the winner. So, what else did we have to vote on besides visibility and popularity? In reality, we should have been selecting a teacher who demonstrated proven results in improving student achievement. Someone who attained 1.5 or 2 years of growth within one year was surely more deserving of a 'Teacher of the Year' title than someone who had the gift of gab and an extraordinary ability to schmooze with leadership...but I digress. Unfortunately, it is NOT uncommon for people working in education to do what is in the best interests of adults (rather than acknowledging and commending those for doing what is in the best interests of students).

But none of the above reasons are why I left education. Actually, I did not leave education at all. Instead, I decided to *TAKE OVER*—and that is what I am here to help you accomplish. If you want to assert your authority in the classroom, the community, and your personal life, then this book was created with you in mind.

Instead of LEAVING education, LEAD IN education!

For help identifying the core competencies and areas of expertise that will position you to lead, visit www.TeacherTakeover.com/toolkit.

With over two decades of experience working in the education sector, I will provide you with tangible strategies for how to lead both inside and outside of the classroom. I will share meaningful pathways that you should consider in pursuit of *The Teacher Takeover*.

The knowledge and resources I will share with you are highly effective. How do I know, you may ask? Because of trial and error. I am living proof. I am not going to share anything with you that I have not applied in some form or fashion to my own professional life.

The content of this book has propelled me from the classroom to the boardroom.

Don't get me wrong—the purpose of this book is NOT to encourage teachers to leave the classroom. Outstanding teachers are absolutely needed in the classroom, particularly if the achievement gap for marginalized students is to ever narrow and close. To the contrary, the purpose of this book is to equip and empower transformational teachers in K–12 education to emerge as leaders within their schools and communities while prioritizing mental health. Anyone striving to enhance the educational trajectory of a child's life will benefit from reading this book.

When I made the difficult decision to leave the classroom, it was because I wanted to have a greater impact outside the walls of the school where I worked. I went on to work as an assessment specialist for Fulton County Schools and a literacy coordinator for Atlanta Public Schools. However, my desire to touch the lives of even more students did not stop there. I became a program manager for the Georgia Department of Education, serving students and stakeholders across the state. Today, I am employed in a role that allows me to impact the educational experiences of students both domestically and abroad. I also serve as the first woman of color to represent District IV on the Gwinnett County Public Schools Board of Education. For context, Gwinnett County Public Schools (GCPS) is one of the largest school districts in the United States, bolstering approximately 182,000 students and an annual budget currently exceeding $3 billion. Getting to this point in my career was no walk in the park, but it would be my pleasure to assist you in manifesting your professional goals.

- If you want to create more opportunities for your students and their families to succeed, this book is for you.

- If you want to impact change within your school, district, or local community, this book is for you.

- If you desire a work-life balance, this book is for you.

As you embark on your transformational leadership experience, the TAG framework depicted in Figure 1 will be a beacon of light. In true teacher fashion, I chose to name the framework with the end in mind. There are three pathways to impactfully disrupt the status quo in public education: Traditional Leadership, Advocacy, and Governance (hence the name TAG). The foundational framework components of Attitude & Authenticity, Be the Expert, and Cultivate Community should be developed simultaneously in preparing to lead for impact. Empowered with the appropriate mindset, knowledge base, and network of supporters, disrupting systems in pursuit of educational excellence will be more attainable. If you take the time to read and apply the information presented in this text, you will achieve notable results within months.

Figure 1. TAG Framework: Lead Impactfully to Transform Outcomes in Education

DISRUPT THE STATUS QUO Traditional Leadership Advocacy Governance		
ATTITUDE & AUTHENTICITY	**BE THE EXPERT**	**CULTIVATE COMMUNITY**
Remain Student-Focused Hold High Expectations Be Solutions-Oriented Demonstrate Empathy	Identify Your Purpose Pursue Higher Education or Targeted Learning Experiences Engage in Professional Development	Seek a Mentor Train and Educate Others Join Alumni and Affiliation Groups Publish Content

The days of waiting for Super(wo)man to save the day are long gone! The time for *THE TEACHER TAKEOVER* is now. Together, we will change the state of the teaching profession. On the other side awaits a more welcoming and enjoyable work environment. This work won't be easy, but it will be well worth it...and best for kids!

CHAPTER 1

Mass Exodus

When I started teaching in the state of Georgia in 2002, my starting salary was $35,500, if memory serves me right. As a recent college graduate not accustomed to paying bills regularly, I was excited to be making "so much money." It allowed me to purchase a one-bedroom apartment minutes away from Lenox Mall. I thought I was doing BIG things because Lenox was (and remains) a high-end shopping establishment with stores such as Louis Vuitton, Armani Exchange, Bloomingdale's, Fendi, Chanel, and let's not forget about Prada. Now, could I afford to shop at those stores...? That is a very different story, but if you're a public school teacher, you already know the answer. Anyway, I was also able to pay the note on a brand-new car. I remember it like yesterday, going down to the lot and picking out a silver 2002 Nissan Altima. That car was my pride and joy for a little over ten years. I didn't ride it until the wheels fell off, but I did keep it until my obsession with having a built-in navigation system won over.

As a first-year teacher, I was also able to partake in entertainment with friends. I particularly liked going to open-air concerts to listen to instrumental music while enjoying the Atlanta weather. Another favorite pastime was meeting up with other teacher friends for drinks and eats so we could vent about that day's/week's/year's hot topic at school. Those conversations could go on for HOURS, and they often did. If you are a teacher, you definitely understand. I remember limiting my time out with friends during the week because, let's be honest, most teachers are exhausted when they get home from work! When you wake up early, work late, and teach with all you've got, there isn't much left in the tank at the end of the day. Nevertheless, I was fulfilled as a novice teacher.

What my younger self didn't know, as a teacher just starting my career, was that my annual salary would only slightly increase from year to year, if at all. I wouldn't be afforded the luxury of buying a home minutes away from Lenox Mall, or even miles away for that matter, because I simply couldn't afford it. And don't even get me talking about travel! I was lucky to go on one vacation outside of the country, and typically, that was to Jamaica or Mexico. The thought of visiting more remote destinations seemed a bit out of reach, or it at least required intentional budgeting over an extended period of time. Oh, and before I forget, did I mention that I had to take on a part-time job at Sylvan Learning Center within my first year of teaching? Yeah, as it turns out, $35,500 wasn't enough to maintain what I considered to be a modest lifestyle—especially once the repayment of my student loans kicked in.

The world should not be surprised that teachers are leaving the field of education in unprecedented numbers. Yes, I said the world. There is an international phenomenon of mass exodus from the schoolhouse due to inadequate pay, the influence of politics, and the lack of respect for the profession altogether. Let's dig into each of these causes in a bit more detail.

Inadequate Pay

During my teacher tenure, there were times when salaries were frozen as a result of financial shortages. For example, you may recall we experienced a nationwide recession in 2008. During that time, it seemed logical that teachers would not receive a pay raise. However, what was not only illogical but also a poor display of empathy for those in the trenches was the superintendent being offered and accepting a $15,000 pay raise. This is the story of former DeKalb County School System Superintendent Crawford Lewis. I remember attending the faculty meeting like it was yesterday. All the teachers in the school were shuffled into the media center. Our principal at the time announced that all employees would not only be denied a pay raise but would furthermore be forced to take a cut in pay and benefits. To say it added insult to injury is an understatement. Talk about a blow to staff morale.

Twenty-two years later, the starting teacher salary in the district where my career began is now $54,735. That's an increase of less than $20K. If rounded up, it's an annual increase of just 3%. What other professional industry has experienced such slothful growth in salary offerings? To be clear, we are talking about the starting teacher salary in the city of Atlanta in the year 2024. This is a place where the typical value of a home is $386,122, according to the Zillow Home Value Index. In 2015, the typical home cost was $207,687. Rounded up, that is an annual increase of 7%. Now, if a teacher's salary only increases by 3% annually and the cost of housing increases by 7%, a dire problem presents itself. There is a teacher workforce that cannot afford to live in the area in which they are employed.

The housing dilemma illustrated is not an isolated phenomenon solely taking place in the city of Atlanta. Teachers across the country are forced to live miles and miles away from the communities they serve. How much more powerful would it be if teachers could actually reside in the same (or at least an adjacent) neighborhood as their students? Staff would encounter lived experiences mirroring those of their students, making it easier to relate to families and empathize where applicable. I was fortunate enough to learn early in my career that "People don't care what you know until they know that you care." When educators demonstrate empathy, students achieve, and parents or caregivers engage at higher levels.

Inadequate pay impacts multiple other areas of life when it comes to livelihood. I remember being pregnant with my first child. In addition to experiencing the joys of becoming a mother, I was burdened with the pains of navigating how to provide for my growing family on a teacher's salary. By this time, I had attained two degrees in an effort to leverage my career. In doing so, I'd also incurred additional student loan debt. To be honest, I felt like I was a hamster running laps on a wheel to nowhere. As a professional with a master's degree, I never imagined I would feel the need to apply for nutritional assistance, better known as food stamps, but I did. To this day, I contemplate how my need as a professional with two degrees competed with the need of someone who perhaps was not even a high school graduate. How is it that one can go to college (after being urged to do so by parents, teachers, counselors, etc.), graduate magna cum laude, and still end up in line applying for government assistance? It's not that I had too much pride to seek the assistance; the real issue is that, as a country, we pay teachers—those responsible for developing the minds of future doctors, lawyers, scientists, and other professionals—so little that they require government assistance. Imagine the toll this takes on a teacher's mental health. After pouring into the lives of so many other people's children and families, imagine experiencing a feeling of deficit when it comes to providing for your own. Teachers should not have to endure this hardship.

The Influence of Politics

Believe it or not, there was once a time when teachers could read a book to their students without the threat of being terminated. Educators could likewise teach:

- history without omitting the facts,

- character development without being told it is outside the purview of schooling,

- and sex education (not restricted to just abstinence) to inform students on how to protect themselves in a comprehensive way.

Katie Rinderlie, a 10-year veteran teacher in Cobb County, Georgia, was fired by the school board in June 2023. She was terminated for reading the book, "My Shadow is Purple," purchased from the school book fair. The majority of the Board chose to override the recommendation of a panel of three educators. Katie is the first teacher to be fired in response to Georgia House Bill 1084. Commonly referred to as the divisive concepts law, the Bill legislates that teachers cannot indoctrinate or persuade a student. Divisive concepts written into the language of the bill focus specifically on racial superiority, racism, and oppression. "My Shadow is Purple" is a book about challenging gender stereotypes. Was Katie supposed to know that reading a book about gender fluidity was not allowed under the new law that was passed only two years prior? The city of Atlanta, just 15 minutes down the road, consistently receives a perfect score of 100% on the Human

Rights Campaign's Municipal Equality Index, which measures the inclusivity of services, laws, and policies within a city pertaining to lesbian, gay, bisexual, and transgender people. One might assume that local politics would support a reading of "My Shadow is Purple" in the classroom. Thinking more broadly, what other concepts are considered divisive and could result in termination if read aloud in the classroom?

To be clear, I am not taking a stance on whether Katie was right or wrong in reading the text to her students. Instead, I am advancing that, in light of the role of politics in today's classrooms, educators ought to be better supported in understanding the laws and policies impacting their profession. Furthermore, they should be provided more granular guidance on what may and may not be considered acceptable practice.

Let us not overlook the fact that Katie had been teaching for TEN WHOLE YEARS. This likely means that she had developed a productive relationship with students, families, other school staff, and external community members. We can assume that her evaluations were favorable over the years, which further implies that her students were making adequate student progress. As an employee of a school system that heralded student success as its mission, one might conclude that Katie Rinderlie had been consistently meeting the mark for the last decade. Thus, it appears Cobb County experienced a tremendous loss when it chose to terminate one of its veterans, particularly at a time when so many teachers are leaving (and college students choosing not to enter) the profession.

Lack of Respect for the Teaching Profession

What if I told you that there is a positive relationship between teacher respect and student achievement? Well, this has been proven to be absolutely true. Research conducted across multiple countries has concluded that there is a CLEAR positive correlation between academic achievement and teacher status or respect. Some indicators used to measure the overall respect of teachers include what teachers should be paid, whether children were encouraged to enter the profession by their parents, and how teachers were viewed relative to other occupations.

The way teachers are perceived in a country informs not only WHO decides to become a teacher but also HOW EFFECTIVE those in the role will be at getting students to learn. Let that sink in for a moment. In a time where news stories are riddled with the declining rate of student performance across literacy and math, not enough attention has been placed on the respect (or lack thereof) given to the workforce and the resulting implications.

Now, what if I also told you there exists a positive relationship between the level of respect for teachers and the likelihood that parents will encourage their children to become teachers? Again, this is absolutely factual. This also holds true despite pay, meaning if parents perceive a lack of respect for the profession, they will not encourage their children to become teachers regardless of the salary offered. Think back to the opening of this book...teachers are leaving the profession in alarming numbers, AND not enough college students are entering the profession. Did a light bulb go off for you? Our teachers need and DESERVE more respect.

So, what does respect for the teaching profession look like? If you are not a teacher, the first thing I would encourage you to do is ask a teacher. I am sure there is a teacher in your family or network who would greatly appreciate the opportunity to share the realities of their profession with someone who is authentically interested and perhaps motivated to support *The Teacher Takeover*. The lists below are provided as starting points.

How to Show Respect for Teachers

1. Ask how they can be supported...and then deliver.

2. Be timely in responding to teacher requests, whether the answer is no, yes, or somewhere in between.

3. Neither mandate nor expect teachers to spend their own money on classroom and school necessities.

4. Neither mandate nor expect teachers to work more than 40 hours a week without additional pay.

5. Encourage teachers to lead by providing opportunities to serve on committees and councils within the school and broader community.

Ways School Leaders Can Better Show Respect for Teachers

1. Manage classroom size. Research supports that students in smaller class sizes outperform their peers in larger class sizes, even after returning to a large class setting.

2. Elevate teacher voices without the threat of retaliation. Advocate for and create policies or procedures to affirm teachers of their right and responsibility to speak up pertaining to what is best for kids. Cultivate a culture of sharing that will not result in ridicule or mistreatment, no matter the message. Design leadership teams and advisory councils that provide a platform for teachers to authentically engage with decision makers in solutioning around challenges.

3. Protect planning time to avoid teacher burnout. Minimize disruptions to instruction during the school day.

4. Prioritize the safety of staff. Student safety is largely discussed, especially in light of the frequency of school shootings. However, the safety of staff is just as important and due just as much deliberation in budgeting and planning.

5. Be transparent in communication. Change is a constant in public education, and no one likes change except for a wet baby. Be thoughtful in developing your messaging. Show empathy. My mother taught me that it's not always what you say but how you say it. Make no mistake—leaders must be strategic in their exchange of information with those they lead. I assert that the degree to which one masters communication strategies is, arguably, what sets apart a GOOD leader from a BETTER leader from the BEST leader.

For a reflective tool to track progress in showing respect for teachers, visit www.TeacherTakeover.com/toolkit.

We Need Good Teachers to Stay

There is no shortage of reasons teachers should leave the profession. The good news is that people are starting to acknowledge the woes that come with the job and take action to attract and retain teachers. For example, some governors have used their power to increase the starting salary of educators in their state. Principals and district administrators have increased investment in wellness programs to support the physical and mental health of teachers. Stakeholders have begun to push for reversal of legislation that impedes the autonomy of educators and the right of students to receive a true and just education. All of this has happened and IS HAPPENING! There is a shift occurring across the United States and abroad. Non-educators are growing concerned with the state of K–12 education. Now that we have their attention, let's tell them not only what we want but what we must have. And no, this is not a time for negotiation. We are showing up with our list of non-negotiables. The time for *The Teacher Takeover* is NOW.

CHAPTER 2

Define Your Why and Commit to the Heart Work

Nearly 20 years ago, I recall being sold the story that third-grade reading scores would help correctional institutions in the U.S. predict the number of beds they would need in the future. A social media post communicating as much went viral in 2022. What I would later come to find out—much later, actually, and only after intentionally seeking the truth—is that this quote is false. What is true, however, is that 85 percent of youth in the juvenile justice system are illiterate, and 70 percent of adult inmates struggle to read at a fourth-grade level. There is no denying the relationship between illiteracy and crime. Literacy is among the most pivotal civil rights issues of our lifetime.

An effective teacher can impact the trajectory of a student's life. What greater reward is there than to know that you can disrupt the generational curse of poverty that many families experience simply by teaching a child how to read? How well reading is taught influences socio-economic status and overall livelihood. New data from the U.S. Census reveals that child poverty more than doubled in 2022 compared to the year prior, and an uptick in poverty signals an increase in illiteracy levels. Students need sound, impactful reading instruction now more than ever before.

This is my WHY. This has been the WHY to sustain me for over two decades in the education profession. I went back to school and paid out of pocket to become an expert reading teacher specifically because of this WHY. I sacrificed time hanging out with friends and dating as a single person in a new city because of this WHY. I gained a few pounds (maybe more) coming home from class late in the evening and eating peanut butter and jelly sandwiches for dinner because of this WHY. I am by no means encouraging you to make sacrifices in the same way or to the same degree I did. However, should you prepare to make sacrifices? YES. Should you neglect your well-being in the process? ABSOLUTELY NOT.

Your mental health is essential to being an effective educator. The scenario acted out on the plane before takeoff holds true in the classroom—educators must put on their own oxygen mask before attempting to help others. You are probably familiar with the adage, "Hurt people hurt others." Educators need to be physically, mentally, and emotionally sound if they are to show up and meet the varied needs of children every day. Being sound in each of these areas doesn't just happen; intentionality is key. We will explore the significance of mental health further in a later chapter.

Working in education is not just hard work but heart work. If your heart's not in it for the kids and their families, I suggest pursuing another occupation. Sympathy is not what is needed. Instead, we must operate in empathy. To operate in empathy means that you may not have experienced the other person's circumstances personally, but you can recognize and understand the other person's feelings. An empathetic person is in tune with others' emotions. To imagine what students may be thinking and feeling is an essential attribute of a high-quality teacher. As a reminder, people don't care what you know until they know that you care—which leads to *The Teacher Takeover* mindset.

The Teacher Takeover Mindset

I'll be the first to admit that the thought of *taking over* anything can be daunting. When it comes to improving educational outcomes, however, the impulse to stay in your comfort zone and wait for someone else to take the lead must be suppressed. The lives of children and livelihood of communities are on the line.

To follow are core beliefs and values that will empower you in the transformational work ahead. Your mindset will determine how you think, feel, and even respond to situations as you endeavor to disrupt the status quo for student success. Consider this list a baseline because it certainly isn't exhaustive. As you read this section, reflect on your belief system and personal values. Think about which beliefs might be missing from the listed criteria and how those beliefs play a role in overcoming challenges.

Be student-focused. As a teacher or someone who works in the field of education, you should always strive to make decisions that are in the best interests of the students. Not the best interests of parents, not the best interests of administrators, and not even the best interests of other teachers. Student success should be at the forefront of all decision-making—and not just success for the majority of students or success for the smartest students, but SUCCESS FOR EACH AND EVERY STUDENT. No student group should be considered less of a priority when it comes to closing the achievement gap. HIGH EXPECTATIONS MUST BE HELD FOR ALL. Unfortunately, it is common for some pockets of students to be overlooked when analyzing performance data. In particular, if there is a large number of students achieving at elevated levels, those students achieving at the low end may be forsaken. Leaders may choose to allocate resources in a way that rewards or benefits high achievers, as opposed to investing additional resources into the needs of children who require remediation. This type of decision making runs counter to *The Teacher Takeover* mindset. To the contrary, we are a collective of individuals who want all students to experience success, both in the classroom as well as in life. It is this mindset that drives our thoughts, speech, and actions in working as a conduit for positive outcomes in education.

Commit. *The Teacher Takeover* necessitates a commitment to serving others. Disadvantaged students, families, and committees don't need a savior. What they need is someone to empathize with their lived experiences and take action in a way that will improve their circumstances. "How can you improve the circumstances of an individual who is not a part of your family," you may ask? After reading this book, you will have discovered a multitude of ways to engage in the heart work.

Persist. Reclaiming your classroom, school, and mental health is going to require persistence. You will have to commit to staying the course despite the varied obstacles, barriers, and challenges presented. Not everyone will support you or your cause. Some will actually oppose what you represent...and that's okay. In fact, it's to be expected. As one of my former school principals told me, "It's time to put on your big-girl panties." In other words, it's a time-out for playing and placating others.

Consider it your duty. The ultimate mindset I compel you to embrace is this: *IF NOT YOU, THEN WHO?* As a teacher, you spend more time with children than almost anyone else. Students are in an elementary classroom for nearly 7 hours a day, Monday through Friday. Unfortunately, parents who work a full-time job are likely unable to spend that amount of time with their children during the workweek. And let's not overlook the fact that many caregivers are now forced to work multiple jobs just to provide the minimum essentials for their family, resulting in even less time available to spend with children. As an example, I recall dropping my kids off at a daycare center around 6:45 am so I could make it back to the center at 3:30 pm to take my daughter to gymnastics practice, which ended around 5:30 pm. That then left me with less than 3 hours to get dinner prepared, assist with homework, read aloud a story for pleasure, and get the kids washed up for bed—just to do the same thing all over again the next day. I was spending approximately four hours a day with my children during the workweek. Their teachers were spending nearly twice as much time with them.

My point is this: Teachers spend an extraordinary amount of time with children and are therefore positioned to learn their wants and needs firsthand. The exposure to student lives which is granted to teachers equips them with a depth of knowledge that no other group possesses outside of the students' families. This is a gift. A number of mothers and fathers wish they could be more available for their children, but the rat race will not allow it. Good teachers understand the importance of developing relationships with their students. Great teachers cultivate an environment where students feel they belong and can be themselves. The relationship between a teacher and student is unique and unlike any other. As a teacher, you have insight into children's lived experiences and feelings that they may not share with anyone else. I urge you to consider it *YOUR DUTY TO SPEAK UP ON BEHALF OF WHAT IS BEST FOR STUDENTS.*

But what if you don't? What if you remain paralyzed by the fear of imposter syndrome? What if you continue to detrimentally trust that someone else is doing a great job making decisions for students? Honestly, I am afraid to think about what other policies and practices might be introduced in our schools and classrooms if teachers choose not to take over. As teachers, you are on the frontline, educating students and working with caregivers day in and day out. You are experts that should be consulted on best practices for students. The voices of low-income communities and people of color are traditionally marginalized in our society—a form of malpractice that you can help eradicate. In the absence of your voice, the flame representing the future of education will continue to flicker dimly when it could spark a fiery blaze. No one is more qualified to shape and craft the educational experience for students than a highly effective teacher. The time to take over is now.

Be the Expert

To be a teacher is one thing, but to take on the role of a change agent is another. There is a tremendous amount of mental gymnastics involved. You will interact with diverse audiences who bring to the table their own mindsets, core beliefs, priorities, and agendas (oftentimes political). What this requires is for you to equip yourself with essential knowledge. Position yourself as the expert in ANY room. Identify what is important to you and become a thought leader that compels others to act. You can accomplish this in a number of ways:

- Read and be current on research to support your cause and dispute the efforts of others who are not acting in the best interests of students.

- Pursue higher education that results in a degree or training that yields additional certification. In the words of my mother, "No one can ever take away your education."

- Connect with a mentor who demonstrates a track record of success in your area of interest.

- Observe and learn from others who have already established themselves as thought leaders and impactful practitioners.

Imposter syndrome is real. I cannot begin to tell you how many times throughout my career I battled with feeling as though I was not the person for the task at hand. What I would soon find out—and rather quickly in those circumstances, after learning the room and hearing the thoughts expressed—is that I was not only qualified to be a thought leader in those spaces, but my experiences equipped me to be one of the more knowledgeable people in the education-centered spaces I occupied. So, whereas others in the room projected opinion as fact, I asserted the truth and unapologetically combated misinformation. More truthtellers are needed in spaces where decisions impacting the lives of children are made.

Find Your People

Taking over anything is seldom an easy task. Instead, it is a feat to be accomplished. I do not encourage you to go at it alone; leveraging a network, whether through professional associations or personal connections, is key to endurance. As a Teach for America alum, I was privy to an abundance of professional learning and teacher development experiences that empowered and surrounded me with others who, likewise, wanted to transform educational outcomes for marginalized students. Connecting with your tribe is arguably the flagship condition leading to longevity in the teaching profession.

Nowadays, you can easily connect with a tribe via social media. Numerous thought leaders and groups exist across various platforms, all of whom are ready to provide teachers with resources, support, and encouragement. Another way to connect with like-minded people is to join a national, state, or local organization that serves teachers. Not only will you meet other educators with similar interests, but you will likely be afforded training to further develop your expertise. Remember, being the expert in the room is essential to taking over. Continuously sharpening your skillset will equip you to lead others over time. You can then establish your own tribe as a thought leader, training others to impact the lives of students and their families.

If you are already teaching, seek out a tribe within your school. There are likely people you work with who have a similar set of values and beliefs when it comes to student success. Forging a relationship with these individuals is essential to your longevity as a teacher. Relationships are often what keep a teacher in the classroom; it certainly is not the pay. Cultivate relationships with other educators, caregivers, and community leaders that help to fill your cup and remind you of the significance of your work. When the obstacles become overwhelming (and at some point, they will), your tribe will be there to guide you through the turmoil. Sometimes your tribe will walk alongside you, and at other times, they may have to push or pull you onward.

What's important is that you have a group of individuals in your circle who are understanding, nurturing, driven, focused, and as dedicated to student achievement as you are.

In the absence of finding your people, students will suffer. It is easy to give in to the pressures that come with teaching when you do not have a network to fall back on. Promising educators with purpose-driven mindsets require the care associated with a collective of people who have experienced similar hardships. Giving up is tempting, and many teachers who join the education profession today will not stay beyond two years. However, it takes more than two years to perfect the craft of teaching. If the schoolhouse is a revolving door for new teachers entering and leaving the profession, our students will never become the beneficiaries of a world-class education. Your people are waiting for you, so find them.

Visit www.TeacherTakeover.com/toolkit for a 1-page summary of the mindset criteria.

CHAPTER 3

Dare to Disrupt
the Status Quo

---

he next few chapters will guide you in becoming a disruptor in pursuit of transforming educational outcomes. The TAG framework (refer to Figure 1 in the book introduction) presents three pathways to impactfully disrupt the status quo: Traditional Leadership, Advocacy, and Governance. Chapter four focuses on the style of school leadership needed to be successful when serving marginalized communities. In chapter five, the concept of advocacy is defined, and educational causes worth advocating are explored. The intricacies of governing a school system are covered in chapter six, along with a thorough discussion of best practices in effective governance.

The following figure is a visual representation of the pathways available to disrupt the status quo as presented in the TAG framework. Traditional leadership is depicted by a paved path representing established authority and hierarchical structures. Advocacy is symbolized as a waterway, indicative of its dynamic nature, often involving grassroots efforts and community engagement. Governance is presented as the grassy pathways sandwiching both the paved road and stream of water. These grassy pathways represent the decisions and policies impacting the work of traditional leaders and advocates alike. It appears that the three pathways will converge at a central point, symbolizing their interconnectedness and shared destination of student success. To download the graphic, visit www.TeacherTakeover.com/toolkit.

Figure 2. Pathways to Disrupting the Status Quo

As you read the next three chapters, be intentional about taking time to reflect on your lived experiences. Consider how you might take steps that will result in meaningful change for students. It doesn't matter whether you are a novice teacher, veteran educator, school staff member, bus driver, parent, caregiver, or concerned community member. No matter your association, you can be a disruptor for educational excellence. The TAG framework exists to support anyone and everyone with advancing student achievement for the betterment of society.

CHAPTER 4
Traditional Leadership

During the first month I was appointed to the schoolwide leadership team at the school where I began my teaching career, I was removed. You have likely heard the age-old adage "truth hurts," and I have never been one to shy away from telling the truth. However, truth-telling does not always sit well with leadership. Truth makes some people uncomfortable, and I concluded this was the case with the principal at my school. Some people would rather avoid the truth than address it. For example, there are sitting legislators who are persistent in their efforts to remove the truth of slavery from elementary and secondary school curricula. These state-elected leaders would rather not talk about this truth and remove it from memory than to take on the hard, heart work of confronting the ills of society, whether past, present, or future. People who would alter, overlook, or deny the truth are not the types of leaders our students need or deserve.

Truthtellers should be invited to have a seat at the table, no matter how uncomfortable it makes others feel. How is an organization to continuously improve if it is not in tune with reality? Despite being removed from the leadership team, I remained committed to my students, their families, and my colleagues. For example, I worked with the school counselor to identify a laundering service for student clothing. I facilitated the launch of a school store to support the real-world application of math skills. I authored a newsletter to strengthen communication with caregivers, ensuring they were aware of how to support learning at home. It was clear that I cared about the community. Ultimately, I was later selected not just to be a member of the leadership team but to serve as co-chair.

This life experience was a teacher. It taught me to stay true to myself and remain authentic, no matter the consequences or challenges. Instead of altering my character, I continued to do what was best for the students. I did not stop speaking my truth. My focus remained set on devising solutions to address the problems that I spoke truth to. It did not matter to me that I wasn't bestowed a formal leadership title. I led. I also worked alongside others to meet the needs of students and their families. At the time, I was enacting what I would later identify through my doctoral studies as *transformational leadership*. Employing a transformational leadership style is essential when in pursuit of better outcomes, particularly for historically marginalized groups.

Transformational Leadership

As a young girl, I was conditioned to play with Cabbage Patch Kids and Barbies. Despite *Transformers* being a popular animated series at the time, I was never able to get my hands on one of the robotic action figures. Understandably so, since it just wasn't something my parents thought to buy for a house full of girls. *Transformers* has since gone on to be developed into a series of blockbuster films jam-packed with captivating action scenes. I am always in awe of how seamlessly the automobiles turn into Autobots on screen, setting out to protect humans. In a similar fashion, transformational education leaders set out to protect students and their families.

When striving to improve outcomes for groups who have been historically overlooked and underrepresented in education, a transformational leadership style is required. Transformational leaders usher in change that results in the organization transcending its current position. Maintaining the status quo yields status quo results. Instead, transformational leaders endeavor to enhance the capabilities and performance of key stakeholders such as students, staff, and parents or caregivers. To transform a school is not an easy task. So, what does it take?

Transformational leaders must have a vision. Having a vision represents the ability to plan the future with imagination and wisdom. Transformational leaders in education are skilled in imagining a future where the needs of historically marginalized populations are met. These leaders are innovative thinkers. They are courageous. They are bold. They do not thoughtlessly continue the traditions and practices that have always been, despite doing so being an easy and comfortable pathway. On the contrary, transformational leaders challenge the status quo. They consider whether the actions employed by the organization meet the needs of stakeholders. If the answer is no, transformational leaders set about establishing a vision, enacting goals, and monitoring progress in their relentless pursuit of improvement. Transformational leaders are cognizant of the need for change and are not afraid to go after it. They perceive barriers as obstacles to be overcome, and they are compelled to take risks. Of utmost importance, high-performing transformational leaders understand that improving people is NOT the goal. The focus is placed on improving policies, processes, and procedures to achieve equitable outcomes. These concepts will be explored further in the chapter on governance. With transformational leaders at the helm, stakeholders are more likely to have the fair access, resources, opportunity, and power required to thrive.

Transformational Leaders are Servant Leaders

Close your eyes and imagine you are at your favorite restaurant. For me, that would be somewhere with a perfectly cooked ribeye or a portion of sea bass seasoned just right. Imagine a server coming to take your order. The server greets you with a smile, asks what you would like, ensures you receive your food hot and in a timely fashion, and makes sure you are happy with your overall dining experience. Some servers are better than others, and these are the waitstaff that take home excessive tip money. What exactly sets the average server apart from a typical server? For me, it is all about attention to detail. I appreciate someone who goes the extra mile and fills my cup before it is totally empty. Or someone who checks in not long after the food is brought to the table to see if any additional condiments are needed. The little things make a BIG difference.

The same is true with school leadership. To thrive as a servant leader means granting attention not just at a high level but also at a microscopic level. A servant leader is in tune with the varied needs within the school. They take the time to seek individualized feedback from stakeholders, whether they be caregivers, students, teachers, or other staff members. They disaggregate the feedback to determine unique areas of opportunity or challenges to be addressed. Servant leaders then align resources (monetary, human, time, etc.) to address the needs of people in an authentic and timely manner. Responding proactively as opposed to reactively should be the goal. You do not want to be seen as someone always putting out fires. Instead, a proactive servant leader establishes herself as forward-thinking and capable of keeping the peace. This attribute helps to elevate the morale of teachers and staff. When staff are happy, they are more likely to return from year to year instead of transferring to another school or district. Consistency in staff develops a strong community within and outside of the school. Parents appreciate having a relationship with the teachers at their local schools, particularly if they have multiple children who will matriculate through the school.

While servant leadership starts at the top, it should not stop there. Everyone on staff, from the cafeteria workers to the bus drivers to the custodians, should embrace a position of service to best meet the needs of historically marginalized communities. There is a foundation of trust that needs to be established and maintained. The desire to partner has to be cultivated, and everyone on staff should be clear on the type of behavior expected and accepted as a member of the team. The leader must define the organizational culture and act as the primary role model. The 'do as I say and not as I do' approach will not yield sustainable results for marginalized communities—and it shouldn't be applied in any school setting, for that matter. Authenticity is essential, as is creating an environment of belonging.

Adaptive Leadership

A transformation-minded educator understands that how she shows up to lead will vary depending on the school's context or situation. Transformational leadership will not look, sound, or feel the same from place to place. To lead effectively requires analysis of the entity's current health alongside the aspirational goals of the organization. A skilled transformational leader must adapt to meet the unique needs presented.

Numerous factors play a role in influencing how a leader should show up to best meet the needs of a school. Three key determinants include:

1. Quality of student outcomes. How are students performing academically? Are students graduating and being promoted as expected? What is the social or behavioral climate?

2. Reputation of the school according to public opinion. Are more families coming to or leaving the school? Are parents satisfied with the school experience and student outcomes? How do students rate the quality of their learning environment and other school factors?

3. Employee morale. Are staff members happy or disgruntled? Do staff speak positively about their work environment and what is expected of them? Do the majority of staff members return to the school each year, or do a high percentage seek employment elsewhere?

Knowing the answers to these questions will inform how leadership SHOULD show up in the space. Let's consider a handful of scenarios in further exploring adaptive leadership.

Scenario #1: Alpha Middle School
Alpha Middle School is situated in a metropolitan school district serving about 50,000 students. The district is very segregated, with most white students attending school on

the north side and black students attending school on the south side. Alpha is on the south side of the city and is designated a Title I school, which indicates that most students live in low-income households. Many of the parents are either unemployed or earn an hourly rate that does not meet the livable wage threshold. Housing and/or food assistance are staples for families that have lived in the area for decades. Many of the students are reading below grade level but somehow manage to advance to the next grade level year after year. Parents typically do not show up for conferences. In talking to some parents, it becomes evident that their personal school experiences were not the best, and they are distrustful of school staff. Discipline concerns are rampant, with bullying and physical attacks becoming commonplace. Teachers in Alpha MS are stressed, burnt out, and at risk of running out of sick leave (often referenced as mental health days in the profession) due to high rates of absenteeism. How should a leader show up in this space?

Scenario #2: Beta Elementary School

Settled in the suburbs bordering a major city, Beta Elementary School has a population that boasts 90% English learners. Most students identify as being Hispanic and have parents who do not speak English. The school is intentional about securing translators for community events, and as a result, parental engagement is astounding. A small percentage of students are considered newcomers and have lived in the United States for less than one year. On the other hand, some students have been in the United

States for quite some time and have older siblings in their families who have mastered the English language. These older siblings often serve as translators for parents, whether engaging with teachers at school or transacting business within the community. Overall, the parents display a willingness to support learning at home and encourage their students to do well. There are minimum discipline issues, with no fights on record for years. Students receive additional language support from trained teachers throughout the day. Statewide test results reveal that the majority of students are reading on grade level. Staff appear to enjoy coming to work and even spend time with one another outside school hours. Teachers collaborate and, with support personnel, meet the needs of students and families. How should a leader show up in this space?

Scenario #3: Delta High School
The graduation rate at Delta High School has been among the top in the state for years. Located in what was once considered a rural area that has undergone a significant amount of development in the last two decades, the student body has shifted from majority white to a balance of more equally represented racial groups. There has been a slight increase in discipline issues reported within the last three years. Parental engagement appears high with a very active Parent-Teacher Organization and School Council. However, some migrant parents express sentiments of not feeling included or welcome in the school. They feel their voices are not being heard. The parents desire more

engagement with school leaders as well as district leadership to ensure the needs of all students are being met. How should a leader show up in this space?

Applying Adaptive Leadership

The scenarios above each require a differentiated approach to leadership. In Scenario #1, there is a need for transformation as it pertains to academic achievement, community trust, and staff morale. There are several opportunities presented for a teacher to lead improvement efforts. For example, the school might benefit from a tutorial program after school, on the weekends, during a scheduled calendar break, or in the summer. Offering parent programs to develop skillsets could both build trust and enhance the employability of those who participate. Addressing the mental health of staff is likewise an area of opportunity. Establishing a designated break room that offers snacks/beverages, a meditation area, and occasional massage services could go a long way. Incorporating mental health breaks for students throughout the day might increase engagement in academics and decrease the occurrence of discipline issues. Leveraging social and emotional development practices could prove to be a successful school-wide initiative spearheaded by a classroom teacher.

In thinking about Scenario #2, all roads appear to be headed toward desired outcomes. To lead in this environment requires the keen ability to look beyond superficial success and aggregate achievement. Peeling back the layers is pivotal. Leaders should disaggregate data results to identify if a particular grade level or demographic of students is not performing on par with peers. Targeted supports should then be put in place to elevate progress and dismantle barriers. Because most parents are Spanish speakers, an English class should be offered if funding is available. Hiring teachers and staff who speak both English and Spanish will add value. Helping to bridge the communication gap between schools and families is paramount. Leaders should likewise offer a workshop to explain the American school system to parents who are new to the country. Topics covered might include school attendance, student code of conduct, graduation requirements, etc.

Leaders in scenario #3 are challenged with maintaining high levels of performance in the face of changing student demographics. Building and sustaining quality relationships with students and their families should be a priority. Academically, students should see themselves reflected in the curriculum. Students should likewise be exposed to staff, and particularly leadership, who look like them. Emphasis should be placed on hiring a diverse staff to mirror the diversity of the student population. The power of extracurricular clubs, sports, and other activities that cultivate team spirit should be leveraged to maximize student engagement outside of the classroom. Parents should be informed of the parent-teacher organization, school council, volunteer opportunities, and other ways to get involved at school. The school should consider partnering with the district to form a parent advisory council that will facilitate two-way communication in addressing the concerns of parents who feel otherwise overlooked.

Adaptive leadership is pertinent to success. The ideas expressed in the previous section are not intended to be an exhaustive list of leadership approaches to be considered. Remember, transformational leadership requires innovative thinking, and transformational leaders take risks. As you take on the challenge of improving student outcomes, be open to considering nontraditional or unfamiliar solutions.

One fundamental tool that has proven to consistently empower leaders across varied organizations is SWOT (strength, weaknesses, opportunities, and threats) analysis. Administering a SWOT analysis helps illustrate an accurate picture of the school environment. Taking the time to understand the current practices and conditions of an organization should be done well in advance of activating any strategy. Implementing change for the sake of change is highly discouraged; doing so often results in diminishing levels of satisfaction among stakeholders. Instead, a communication plan should be put in place to explain changes to stakeholders, along with the rationale for those changes and their intended outcomes. Fostering buy-in as early as possible is vital. School leaders should be intentional about engaging students, parents, caregivers, and community members in the needs assessment process. After all, those affected by school decisions are likely most adept at identifying sustainable solutions. For a sample SWOT analysis template, visit www.TeacherTakeover.com/toolkit.

The Truth About Leadership

Leadership can be lonely. Why, you ask? I had the same question as a first-year graduate student at Clark Atlanta University. I could not quite wrap my head around the concept of why someone leading masses of others would ever feel alone. The media typically portrays leaders as being surrounded by others and interacting with various stakeholders routinely. However, the mere presence of people does not equate to togetherness—or even solidarity, for that matter. You can be in a room full of folks and still feel alone.

Leaders are visionaries. They are innovators. They do not stop at seeing things the way they are but see things the way they COULD and SHOULD be. This way of thinking can be a lonely state. Being a trailblazer is not an easy decision to make. Now, some may choose to lead and maintain the status quo; such leadership does not require much thought and will not yield progress. If you are reading this book, then you are not that type of leader. You know that there is much progress to be had across a spectrum of issues. So, for you, my friend, do not expect leadership to be a glamorous, fun-filled adventure. Nevertheless, accept the challenge. Leading is worth whatever comes your way if it means better outcomes for students, especially those continually marginalized and overlooked.

Everyone's path to leadership will differ. Your work and dedication will speak for you and attract leadership opportunities. Careful thought should go into which leadership roles you choose to accept. You want to lead within an organization that has values that align with your own. Diversity of thought should be heralded and embraced. Transparency in communication is key to not only developing relationships but to sustaining them in a manner that yields productivity. And, while I caution you not to be an open book at all times, it is also important to show your humane side to those you work alongside. Share your hobbies, interests, accomplishments, and goals outside of work life. Maybe it is biking, perhaps you write novellas, or better yet...perhaps you have starred in a novella! The point is that when people get to know you as a person (and not just as a leader), they are more likely to connect with you. If cultivated, this can result in maximal levels of productivity. Just as importantly, you should strive to know those you lead on a personal level. People don't care what you know unless they know that you care. I cannot stress this idea enough to those in pursuit of transformational leadership.

Teacher Takeover Testimonial

I have had the distinct privilege of being mentored and supported by Dr. Simmons. Her leadership style, rooted in empathy, strategic vision, and a commitment to equity, has not only guided her in her role but also profoundly impacted my personal and professional journey.

At the heart of Dr. Simmons' leadership style is a deep sense of empathy. She approaches her role on the school board with genuine concern for the well-being of students, teachers, and the broader community. This empathy is not just a passive trait but an active force that drives her decision-making process. She listens attentively to the concerns of all stakeholders, ensuring their voices are heard and needs met.

This quality has been a cornerstone of her mentorship to me. She has consistently offered a listening ear and thoughtful advice in moments of doubt or challenge. Her ability to understand my experiences and challenges, both personal and professional, has been invaluable. She does not merely provide solutions but helps me navigate the complexities of my circumstances, always considering how decisions might impact the broader community.

Dr. Simmons' leadership is also characterized by a strategic vision anchored firmly in a commitment to equity. As a board member, she is acutely aware of the disparities that exist within the educational system and works tirelessly to address them. Her decisions are guided by a desire to create an environment where every student has the opportunity to succeed, regardless of their background.

This vision has inspired me in my work within education. Through her example, I have learned the importance of looking beyond the immediate to consider the long-term implications of decisions. Her mentorship has taught me to approach challenges with a strategic mindset, always asking how I can contribute to creating a more equitable and just educational system.

Perhaps the most profound impact Dr. Simmons has had on me is through her unwavering support as a mentor. She has been a source of strength and encouragement, helping me grow personally and professionally. Her belief in my abilities has often been the push I needed to pursue opportunities from which I might have otherwise shied away.

Her support is not limited to offering advice or guidance; she actively invests in my success. Whether it's through connecting me with resources, providing constructive feedback, or simply being there to celebrate my achievements, she has played an instrumental role in my development. This mentorship has not only enhanced my professional skills but bolstered my confidence, enabling me to take on new challenges with greater assurance.

Dr. Simmons' leadership style has shaped the way I approach my work, my relationships, and my aspirations.

Her empathy, strategic vision, and commitment to equity have become guiding principles in my own life. Through her mentorship, I have gained not only a deeper understanding of what it means to be a leader but also a clearer sense of purpose.

In a world where effective leadership is often hard to come by, I am incredibly fortunate to have such a remarkable friend and mentor. Her example serves as a constant reminder of the power of empathy, the importance of strategic thinking, and the necessity of equity in all endeavors. As I continue on my journey, I do so with the confidence and knowledge that her mentorship has provided, and for that, I am grateful.

Yolunda Baskins
Instructional Coach

CHAPTER 5
Advocacy

M aybe it did for you, but a chapter on advocacy didn't exist in my textbook as I was learning to become a teacher. My classmates and I spent a great deal of time exploring how to teach reading, writing, and arithmetic, but discussions around advocacy were, I assume, deemed less important. As a transformational leader, I cannot think of a more important topic.

Advocacy Defined

Educational advocacy is the driving force that ensures students and families have access to much-needed resources and support. To be an advocate is to strive to make a difference in someone's life. Advocates are public in their support of causes, working to improve the well-being of others in need. An advocate makes known to others her stance on issues and recommendations on how to solve problems. Advocates assist people in understanding their rights and connect people to resources to help alleviate or resolve their burdens. To advocate effectively requires a knowledge base rooted in fact, simultaneously architectured with historical context and current research. Heed these words and always remember:

Not everyone who advocates does so in truth. And when it comes to education, not everyone who advocates does so in the best interests of students.

Many people advocate for causes in education that are in the best interests of adults, clients, or whoever is paying the most money. Greed can undoubtedly cloud one's judgment. Unfortunately, the end result is often maintenance of the status quo or a lack of change to substantially move the needle for students who are already marginalized and not meeting academic expectations.

Advocate-worthy Causes in Education

The number of issues that students and their families are challenged with each day can be mind-boggling. So, how do you narrow down which causes to advocate for, considering time limitations and the level of effort you are able to give? Most importantly, you should identify an issue that is of personal interest. There's nothing like running into someone who considers herself an advocate but lacks passion when speaking on the topic. You want to grab hold of a cause that resonates with your values. You do not have to personally be impacted by the issue, but you should be concerned about those who *are* impacted. Furthermore, you should know their stories by engaging with the impacted community in a way that provides exposure and deepens experience.

During my junior year of college, I decided to change my major. Yes, I was one of those students! At the time, I had concluded that a career in accountancy was no longer my goal. I had no desire to crunch numbers on a spreadsheet all day for the next thirty-plus years of my life. As fate would have it, I had begun tutoring a young autistic boy, who we will refer to as Sam, in the fall of that year as a way to make more money. Although I had received a pretty substantial academic scholarship to attend the University of Missouri, it wasn't a full scholarship, so I needed extra money to make ends meet. I remember Sam being a gentle spirit who loved spending time outdoors. On the surface, he appeared like any other elementary school-aged boy. However, he was socially different in a number of ways. This difference, however, did not limit his ability to learn, and in my mind, learning would serve as somewhat of an equalizer for him. I went about supporting Sam (I suppose as best a 20-year-old could without years of educational training) in mastering social, emotional, and academic tasks. The empowerment he displayed during the semester we spent together, coupled with the undeniable joy that I experienced, convinced me that a career in education was my calling.

Not long after I began working with Sam, I recall walking across campus and seeing a huge poster plastered across one of the university columns tagged with the words "Teach for America." I was immediately intrigued. Up until that point, I had never heard of Teach for America, more casually known as TFA, so I began to do some research. What I would find out was that the organization was (and continues to be) fueled by the belief that "one day, all children will have the opportunity to attain an excellent education." This vision resonated with me over 20 years ago, and it still serves as a guiding light in my personal pursuits.

What started as a walk across the commons area on the campus of my alma mater led to me choosing a career in public education upon graduation. I spent five years teaching first and third graders in Atlanta Public Schools. The school where I was assigned to teach for my first year was undergoing renovations. In the meantime, we were placed in an old building that appeared dilapidated in many areas—it certainly was not a place where I would want my child to attend school. There wasn't enough space for each teacher to have her own classroom, so I shared a room with another teacher. That meant double the amount of students in an already cramped space. Our room was adjoined to yet another teacher's classroom, requiring the students of three classes to enter and leave from the same door each day. Imagine the foot traffic and level of noise in that space. It was nearly impossible to get through a lesson without some sort of disturbance, and teaching time was undoubtedly impacted. Subsequently, that meant that learning time was also negatively impacted. Despite the circumstances, my peers and I did the best we could to foster a culture of care and belonging that would ultimately set the stage for high academic achievement.

The exposure and experience I acquired as a Teach for America educator cemented in me the importance of establishing lofty goals and maintaining elevated expectations for each and every student. Despite the unappealing surroundings and subpar teaching conditions, our students needed to learn. Not only did they need to learn, but some of them needed to learn 1.5 to 2 years of academic content within one year if they were to go to the next grade level adequately prepared. As you can imagine, this was no easy feat. However, it was attainable. Overcoming the odds continues to be attainable; it just requires relentless pursuit, innovative thinking, disciplined action, and the willingness to take risks.

My time teaching in the general education classroom and thereafter leading in other educational roles informed the following list of what I consider to be advocate-worthy causes in academia. When putting the list together, what struck me was alignment of the causes with Maslow's Hierarchy of Needs. Maslow posits that our needs are what motivate us, and the most basic level of need is physical survival. If physiological needs are not met, the body cannot function. All other needs, as presented in Figure 3, are therefore secondary. As needs are fulfilled, individuals become motivated to secure the needs of the next level up. Some, however, believe that the order is not fixed and behavior can be motivated by multiple needs at once.

Figure 3. Maslow's Hierarchy of Needs

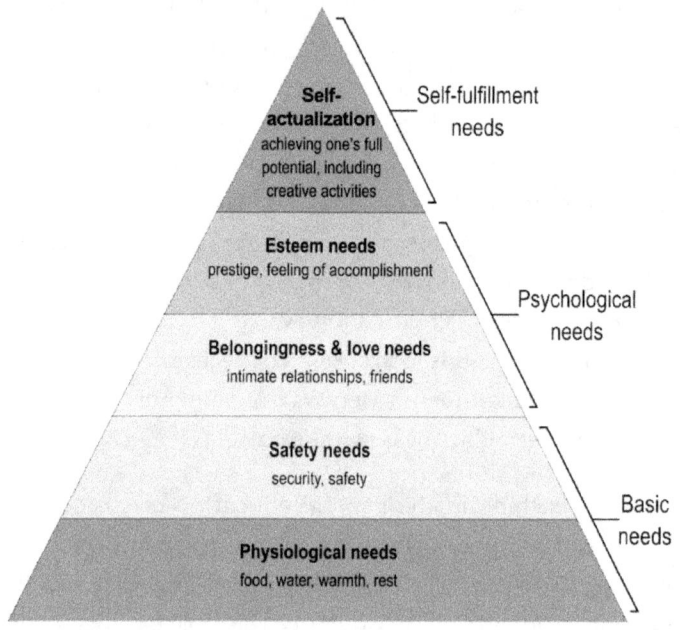

The following advocate-worthy causes in education are presented in order of motivational need. This list is not exhaustive. In determining which causes you should advocate, think about the issues most familiar to you. Perhaps you know a student with a disability who is facing educational challenges, or maybe homelessness is a growing concern where you live. Numerous life circumstances affect and impede the ability to learn. That does not mean, however, that learning is impossible. On the contrary, learning can indeed occur if there is intentionality in overcoming challenges—hence the need for advocates.

Food and Clothing Stability. Imagine for a moment students entering your classroom on a Monday morning. Most come in bubbly and chattering about their weekend. However, one (we'll call him Xavier) enters the room with a glum look and does not appear interested in socializing. As the teacher, you approach Xavier to initiate small talk. Before you can spark up a conversation, you notice a foul odor surrounding the space Xavier occupies. The smell does not stop you, of course, from asking Xavier about his weekend. During the conversation, you casually ask Xavier if he would like a cereal bar. He immediately responds yes and gobbles it down. His demeanor appears to lighten a bit as you prepare to lead the class in a math lesson.

This scenario is not unfamiliar in low-income communities. I previously shared my experience of collaboratively working to secure laundering services to clean student clothing. I vividly recall one instance when a student came to school, day after day, wearing a pair of socks with a very pungent stench. The smell coming from his socks was so overwhelming that it impacted the ability of the class to learn and my ability to teach. This detail is not shared to disparage anyone. Instead, as a truthteller, I am making clear a barrier to learning that is likely unknown to the masses. Some assert that it is not the role of a teacher to ensure children's clothes are washed and that this is a home issue. However, most (if not all) teachers will tell you that home and school are inseparable in many cases. What happens at home ABSOLUTELY impacts what educators can accomplish at school.

Empathetic school leaders—those who get it—often go the extra mile by offering hygiene products and clothing not only to students but to their families as well. As it pertains to food security, the federal government provides free breakfasts and lunches to students whose families meet a certain household income threshold. There are many families, however, that do not meet the requirements for their students to receive free food. Caregivers may be required to pay a reduced price for meal services. But what happens when the caregiver does not pay for school meals as required?

In local news recently, a school district announced that students who had unpaid balances on their food accounts would be served cheese sandwiches every day moving forward until their debts were paid. This announcement led to an outcry among community members. Within days, concerned citizens had raised almost $100,000 to pay off the debt of all students. Individual donors were subsequently refunded as a result of a corporate grant offered by a fast-food entity's foundation to eliminate the debt balances.

Life circumstances often present as barriers in the academic setting that must be overcome. Transformational leaders do not allow life circumstances, especially those outside the control of the student, to impede learning. Just like we invest in support for students who are mentally disabled, a hefty investment should be made to support students living in poverty. A student who is well-fed and adequately clothed is more likely to engage in the learning process. When physical needs are met, the ability to focus is strengthened. If we want students to achieve at high levels, we must *FIRST* ensure that their basic needs are met.

Safety and Security. Those who work in education tend to align with parents in their belief that safety and security should be the number one priority of schools. Over the last decade or so, the idea of providing security in schools has broadened to not only focus on the children but also on protecting school staff. Within the first five days of the new year in 2024, there were already four school shootings in the United States. That's an average of about one school shooting per day! The previous year, we experienced more than 300 school shootings.

As a parent myself, there is nothing more important than my kids returning home unharmed at the end of the day. Students may complain of a horrible lunch or a mean teacher...but those are issues that can be addressed in partnership with school administrators. However, what cannot be sorted out with any level of school district staff is the death of a child. It is pertinent that school leaders invest in systems to cultivate an environment of comfort and safety for their students and staff. There was once a day in age when considerable funding did not need to be designated toward securing school buildings. Now, a lack of investment could result in the loss of lives. There is no undoing death or the type of psychological harm that survivors will be forced to live with for the rest of their lives.

There are various security features you can advocate for to keep students and staff safe. For example, school districts across the country are implementing danger alert systems. Under this system, staff members wear badges inclusive of a panic button that, when activated, will alert school leaders to their exact location. Whether inside the building or on the perimeter of campus, the system enables immediate attention to be rendered in the case of emergencies. Another security feature becoming more and more prevalent across schools is that of a door entry system. This particular system regulates access inside a property, meaning individuals are granted or prevented entry into the school building. In some cases, identification credentials must be provided before entry is granted. Sex offenders and other unwelcome individuals are immediately identified and denied entry into the property. There are certainly a lot more systems that leaders can put into place to foster a greater sense of security within the school community.

Mental Health. Psychological needs are presented next in priority after basic needs in Maslow's Hierarchy of needs. When thinking about the number of shootings that have occurred and continue to occur in American schools, it is impossible not to conclude that mental instability is a key driver behind the shooters' behaviors. Schools have been serving the social and emotional needs of learners for years. As a matter of fact, school counselors are charged with promoting academic, career, and social/emotional development. They are instrumental in helping students apply interpersonal skills and manage their emotions. Beginning in the elementary grades, counselors routinely meet with learners to implement guidance lessons on topics such as relationship building, decision making, communication, and conflict resolution. Some argue that character development and social-emotional learning should not be taught in school. They believe students should come to school solely to learn how to read, write, and do arithmetic. However, what if a student isn't receiving social and emotional support at home?

In my experience as a classroom teacher and instructional coach for over a decade, students exhibiting behavioral problems, ultimately disrupting classroom instruction, are actually crying out for attention. They are in need of love and a sense of belonging. If teachers want to optimize learning time, it is in their best interests to cultivate environments in which students can learn how to express their feelings and work through conflict appropriately. Assuming that these soft people skills are developed at home can be detrimental to the learning process. The more time teachers spend addressing poor behavior, the less time they spend teaching academic content. Taking the time to develop people skills in students does not only reduce the occurrence of disruptive behavior; it prepares students for life after school, and it prepares youngsters for relationships, both personal and professional. It equips them for success in the workplace and as leaders in their communities. Empowering learners with knowing how to treat others is just as important, if not more so, than teaching them algebra or the saga of Macbeth.

A common phrase currently used in the world of K–12 academia is whole child education. The whole child approach prioritizes addressing a child's full scope of developmental needs, including cognitive, physical, social, emotional, and mental health. Such an approach ensures every child reaches their full potential. Whole child education supports that student learning and life outcomes are dependent upon access to school environments that are safe and welcoming. Furthermore, the humanity of teachers and students is centered in a way that cultivates belonging and connection. Learning environments thrive under these conditions.

Education should not be limited to the scholastic development of children. We should advance beyond defining success solely in terms of academic test performance. Schools should commit to addressing the range of learners' developmental needs through culture, curriculum, instruction, assessment, professional development, and engagement with families and community.

The astonishing reality is that elevated student achievement is just one indicator resulting from a commitment to whole child development. Students will additionally exhibit improvement in attendance, behavior, health, and soft people skills. Whole students are what schools should be striving to produce. Our future deserves citizenship and a workforce that is not only knowledgeable and skilled but emotionally and physically healthy. Such a person represents the epitome of a successful learner. Such a person is prepared for life.

Literacy. Illiteracy always has been and continues to be a global phenomenon. Nearly a billion adults lack basic literacy skills, and most of them are women. Crises such as the COVID-19 pandemic as well as international conflicts have worsened the issue. Shockingly, the problem is not unique to those living in poverty.

So why is learning to read and write so important? Why should it be considered the social rights issue of our time? Simply put, literacy rate is a key determinant of earning potential. The more literate one becomes, the more earning potential realized, which in turn strengthens buying power. Literate people have access to better homes, neighborhoods, schools, and services such as medical treatment. Literate individuals rise above the stressors of home and food insecurity, and their basic needs are met more easily compared to illiterate peers. They are more mentally freed up and motivated to build intimate relationships and develop friendships, both of which are salient components of sound mental health. In reflecting on Maslow's Hierarchy of Needs introduced earlier in the chapter, a literate person can dedicate more time and energy toward physiological need attainment and self-fulfillment.

To impact the trajectory of someone's life, teach that person to read and write.

Think about it: How essential is literacy to everyday tasks that you complete? From receiving and sending emails at work to paying bills, following a recipe, or corresponding with your child's teacher. Comprehension in reading and the ability to write are essential skills in navigating life.

In the absence of literacy, effective communication is arguably impossible. If I come from a low socioeconomic background, the possibility of me not being proficient in reading and writing is substantial. However, what is also substantial is the level of support I need for both me and my family. Now, imagine how complicated the scenario becomes if I pursue resources to meet the needs of my family without possessing the skills to read and write. It is impossible to comprehend the many forms and waivers that must be signed. Numerous barriers are presented. Accessing shelter, securing food and clothing, and landing a job each present as individual challenges. As a reminder, when basic needs are not met, the body cannot function (reference Maslow's Hierarchy of Needs earlier in the chapter). Mental and physical health become threatened. A detrimental, never-ending cycle or chain of events ensues when a child does not learn to read and write. Addressing this issue does not require rocket science; mastering literacy is the answer.

How to Advocate Effectively

Earlier in the chapter, I established that an advocate is someone who publicly supports causes and works to improve the well-being of others. What advocacy looks like in action can take on many forms. At its most basic level, advocacy requires the ability to communicate or at least distribute information. The following are tips to help you get started if you are new to the work of advocacy. The tips are also beneficial as a reference to those who are experienced advocates and should be considered a tool in sharpening your skillset to actively transform people's lives.

1. Know the law and people's rights. Advocacy is required in spaces where the law is not being upheld. While I did not introduce the topic of special education in the list of advocate-worthy causes earlier in the chapter, it serves as a prominent area in need of advocacy. Schools and school systems across the country are guilty of not abiding by the law when it comes to educating children. However, one must first know the law to identify instances where the law is not being followed.

2. Study the issue at hand. Once you have identified a need or problem to advocate for, immerse yourself in news and research to further inform your understanding of the topic. Prepare yourself to answer questions aptly and astutely; this will help to establish and sustain your position as a leader for the cause. Some in the crowd may ask questions to better understand the issue, while others in the crowd may outwardly oppose your stance. Be prepared with facts, data, and even personal or secondhand narratives to detail the intricacies of the problem.

3. Identify your needs and be resourceful. Your advocacy efforts will be more effective if you employ the assistance of others. Identify organizations that support your cause and then partner with them to bring awareness to larger audiences. Build alliances with other individuals who can lend their time or expertise. Understand that serving as an advocate is not characterized as fun and games. On the contrary, there will be moments where your character might be attacked by those with opposing views. History further demonstrates that physical danger is a possibility. Establishing a network of fellow advocates is essential to maintaining your mental health while doing this crucial yet trying work.

4. Determine key audiences and learn them. It is imperative for you to understand the values, interests, or concerns of the people you interact with on the advocacy platform. Identify how to connect with the crowd in order to win them over. As an advocate, you want to compel others to act. One of your ultimate goals is to convert other people into advocates. Doing so amplifies your cause, brings more attention to the issue at hand, and increases the likelihood of those with power doing something to address the problem.

5. Use clear and consistent communication. *Do not misinterpret this to mean that you must be a perfect communicator.* I'm reminded of the biblical

character Moses, who self-proclaimed that he was not eloquent in his speech. The scripture suggests that he may have had a speech impediment; he may have stuttered. Moses was still no doubt an impactful leader among his people. Prepare for speaking opportunities by drafting your talking points. Practice your speech in the mirror. Pay attention to your facial expressions, body language, and gestures, as communication encompasses more than just the words that come out of your mouth. Become skilled in timing long pauses and raising or lowering your voice to bring emphasis to particular parts of your message. And be consistent! The key takeaways of your advocacy message should reverberate across audiences, so know in advance what those key takeaways are. Draft a communication plan as a guide in the early stages of your advocacy efforts, then revisit it as needed.

6. Establish explicit goals and expectations. Otherwise, you will tire yourself out sharing a message with no finish line in sight. There will be no sense of accomplishment and no opportunity to celebrate a win. Work within your network to design an action plan. Concoct a timeline to accompany your plan. I am not suggesting there will be a hard stop to your advocacy efforts, as for many, it is a lifetime pursuit. However, milestones should be established to track the effectiveness of your

efforts. Document your progress and delight in successes, no matter how big or small.

7. Believe in yourself. We often achieve things in life that, when looking back, we did not imagine we would or could. If you ask me how we do it, my response is to not overthink it. Put one foot in front of the other and go. As the old proverb says, "There is only one way to eat an elephant: one bite at a time." Break down your goal into bite-sized pieces so you do not become overwhelmed with the big picture. From there, garner the skills, resources, and courage needed to progress. Don't focus on the challenges…yes, they will absolutely present themselves. Instead, focus on your knowledge, your abilities, and your unique experiences; they have equipped you for the tasks ahead. Reminisce on your past successes as motivation to propel you forward. *You are prepared for such a time as now. If not you, then who?*

Transformation in education will not just happen. Someone must dare to challenge the status quo. Someone must take action to right the wrongs perceived. An advocate is that someone. On issues big and small, advocates serve as the anchor of transformation. Advocates are needed now more than ever to right the wrongs of current-day society. In the essence of Mahatma Gandhi, let us "be the change…[we] wish to see in the world."

Visit www.TeacherTakeover.com/toolkit to download the steps on how to advocate effectively.

Teacher Takeover Testimonial

I had the privilege of meeting Dr. Simmons during my first year of teaching, at a time when I was transitioning from a different school and grappling with the challenges of adjusting to a new environment. I was teaching Kindergarten while Dr. Simmons led the first-grade classroom next door. Her support and mentorship were instrumental in shaping my career as an educator.

Dr. Simmons recognized that my students would potentially become hers the following year, and she approached our collaboration with remarkable patience and kindness. Her constructive feedback was always thoughtful and aimed at helping me grow. One of the most impactful areas she helped me with was classroom management. I struggled to complete all my planned activities by the end of the day, and Dr. Simmons generously opened her classroom for me to observe and learn.

She provided practical suggestions to enhance my daily schedule and shared effective procedures that could streamline my activities. Dr. Simmons didn't stop there; she even took the time to observe my classroom while her own students were at lunch and then offered personalized feedback. Her guidance was invaluable, leading to a significant decrease in wasted time and a more efficient classroom routine.

More than 20 years later, I can trace a substantial part of who I am as an educator back to the support and mentorship of Dr. Simmons. Her dedication and generosity have left a lasting impact on my professional journey, and I am deeply grateful for the role she played in my development.

Marquel Hooks

District Mentor Teacher

CHAPTER 6

Governance

I f you are anything like me, the thought of governing never crossed your mind as a classroom teacher. You are likely busy expending all of your time and energy creating lesson plans, communicating with students and families, grading papers, and completing the required paperwork for the various other exponentially numerous tasks that teachers are bogged down with. Most days, you probably go home exhausted. For you and many other educators, a feeling of exhaustion is often misconstrued as a sign of a productive day. What I have come to learn, however, is that you should not be leaving your all in the classroom.

For one, you should be reserving energy to accomplish personal goals outside of work (which we will talk about in the next chapter). But also, as a transformational educator, you should seek and pursue opportunities to extend your reach outside of the classroom. You have to start somewhere, even if you must do it afraid. I remember serving as a co-chair on our school's design team and being terrified. I had no idea what Robert's Rules of Order were, yet I was to lead the meeting and ensure everyone was following said rules. I did not succumb to the discomfort, and neither should you. Muster up the courage to do it afraid, if necessary. Push aside the imposter syndrome that will surely peak its head. Never in my wildest dreams did I imagine one day using my voice to provide direction for an entire school district. However, today I am doing just that: influencing the public education experience of over 180,000 students and their families.

In 2022, I was elected to the board of education for Gwinnett County Public Schools, one of the largest school systems in the United States. Governing is the epitome of leadership, and more teachers should consider running for the school board. Board members make decisions that directly impact the experiences of students, teachers, staff, and families. Have you identified areas of improvement in your school or school district that need to be addressed? Are you concerned about student achievement or the lack thereof? Well, stop complaining. It is time to take action. You need to pursue a school board seat!

What to Expect as a School Board Member

School governance teams are made up of the board of education (alternatively referred to as the Board) and the superintendent. The Board is responsible for hiring, evaluating, and firing the superintendent. In collaboration, the governance team sets the vision for the entire organization. They also work to approve the annual budget for the school system and enact systemic policies. In a nutshell, the duties of a school board member can be summarized as follows:

1. Select and evaluate the superintendent
2. Approve the budget
3. Devise policies

On the surface, being responsible for *only three things* does not appear to be a heavy lift. *Accomplishing* these three things, though, requires a delicate balance of expertise, skill, and strategy...not to mention political astuteness. Yes, being elected to the board of education involves a great deal of politics. In Gwinnett County, Georgia, I serve alongside four other representatives. In total, five people make up the school board, representing over 180,000 students and their families. As a board, we make decisions based on the vote of the majority. So, with five representatives on the board, at least three people must agree on a matter in order for a decision to be acted upon. Politics therefore comes into play when vying to win over two additional votes to support what you feel to be the best decision. Connecting with fellow board members is paramount. You must take the time to learn about their interests, personal values, and priorities. Doing so empowers you to propose your agenda in the best way possible and garner individualized buy-in.

Consider, for example, the topic of investing in pre-kindergarten (also referred to as pre-K). In Georgia, school systems are not allocated state funds to support pre-K programming. Research, however, posits that students who attend pre-K outperform their peers academically. In a school district where assessment results reveal a decline in reading performance across grade levels, it makes sense to consider investment in pre-K. However, the requirement of a balanced budget means that the Board will need to reallocate the current funds. As a member of the Gwinnett Board and one who believes that pre-K programming is in the best interests of students, you must now campaign to win the vote of at least two other members for a majority vote to pass. In your conversation with other board members, it would help to discuss the following to influence the vote:

- **Does the board member have a child in his family that attended pre-kindergarten?** If so, discuss the child's experiences and how the child was better prepared for elementary school. If not, share your personal experiences coupled with research on the impact of pre-K education on the lives of children.

- **Are their areas currently over-funded in the school system budget?** Identify where spending can be cut so that funds can be reallocated to build a pre-K program.

- **Would you support piloting a pre-K program to examine the results on a small scale before investing on a larger scale?** It doesn't hurt to do homework and experiment before making a huge financial investment. In actuality, it is a good idea to do so. When it comes to pre-K, many organizations have already completed experimentation to prove its effectiveness. Nevertheless, if fellow board members are hesitant, agree to start small and scale over time.

Governing successfully is very much predicated on establishing and sustaining productive relationships. To be in relation with someone requires getting to know that individual. It takes time and effort to truly come to understand another person's motivations. As a politician (and yes, a board member is a politician), you should plan to build relationships not only with those you are elected to serve but also with those you will serve alongside. In the absence of a majority vote that represents your views, power and influence will remain distant aspirations. Impacting transformation in governance cannot be accomplished single-handedly. Because relationships are pivotal to successful governance, we will revisit this topic at length toward the end of the chapter. For now, let's dive into the 5Ps of school board governance.

The 5P Framework of School Board Governance

Leading on a school board is different from other types of elected leadership. In fact, Georgia state law dictates that school board members are not to be treated in the same way as other elected officials due to the role's unique nature. So, what makes membership on a local school board so special? That is where the 5P Framework comes into play. There are five distinct categories of dynamics that board members must consistently navigate in the role: Power, Policy, Procedures & Processes, and People. We will start our discussion of the 5P's beginning with power. To download a summary of the 5P Framework for School Board Governance, visit www.TeacherTakeover.com/toolkit.

Power

Getting elected to serve on a school board in today's climate can be a bit tricky. In 2021, Gwinnett County tossed aside its decades-long tradition of holding a partisan election during the general election period in favor of a nonpartisan election during the primary cycle. Why would an establishment choose to do such a thing, considering voter turnout during the primaries is a small fraction of the turnout during the general election? Well, what it boils down to is an attempt to maintain power.

For as long as Gwinnett County has had a school board, it has been run by the Republican Party. Within the last 10 years or so, however, the county has become what pundits consider a 'purple' locale, meaning more democrats have moved into the area. Republicans are now a minority in many parts of the county. In 2018, the Gwinnett County Public School Board of Education welcomed its very first Democrat, who also happened to be black. To date, all other members on the board had been white Republicans. Imagine the shock when this shift occurred. The following cycle, in 2020, two more democrats were elected to the Board. This now meant that Democrats made up the majority. One of the first orders of business for the now Democrat-led board was to remove the longest-serving superintendent in U.S. history. Boy, oh boy, did this decision ruffle many feathers. Shortly thereafter, state legislators made the school board election nonpartisan, meaning candidates no longer declared whether they were Republican or Democrat. The school board election was also moved from the November general election ballot, when most constituents turn out to vote for the president of the United States, to the May primary election ballot. This past 2024 election cycle, less than 20% of registered voters turned out to vote in the primary election. In numerous electoral districts, less than 10% of registered voters turned out to vote. A runoff was required for two of the board seat races, requiring voters to once again come out in June. Approximately 6% of registered voters came back out to vote in one race and just above 3% in the other.

Many deduced that the intent of changing the school board election process was to return power to the Republicans. This strategy failed in my case. I was elected to the GCPS school board in June 2022 as the first black woman to represent District IV, and I am a Democrat.

A pivotal question remains: Does it matter whether a school board is partisan or nonpartisan? The reality is that the attitudes, beliefs, principles, and decisions of *people*, despite their political party alignment, determine the productivity and effectiveness of a body that governs. We will further explore the significance of people within the governance structure in a later part of the chapter.

Policy
Local boards of education are responsible for setting policies that lead to the operational success of school systems. So, what exactly is a policy? A policy is a principle or course of action adopted by a governing body. Policies are the guardrails applied to the practices of an organization. If you think about the purpose of guardrails, they serve to keep

commuters out of harm's way, and they prevent drivers from veering off the road. Essentially, guardrails serve to keep those in control of vehicles on a straight path. Organizations need policies for the same reason. Policies help keep businesses out of the danger zone. They exist to provide structure as to how the company will operate. Policies should not be specific to the point that they do not allow for flexibility in implementation. However, they should be detailed enough to make clear what behaviors are acceptable or unacceptable.

In GCPS, our school board policies are grouped into eleven categories, inclusive of school district organization, school board operations, general school administration, fiscal management, business management, personnel, students, and instructional programs. We even have a policy that requires the Board to review and reaffirm policies on an annual basis. The Board must ensure policies are in compliance with and reflect changes to state legislation as well as state board rules and regulations. In the absence of updating policies to remain current with the law, school districts risk losing their accreditation. This is the absolute worst thing that can happen to a school district. The district may no longer be eligible for funding, and this would result in the reduction or outright elimination of programming. The loss of accreditation may also prevent teachers from receiving benefits. While school accreditation is voluntary, colleges typically require diplomas from accredited high schools. If a K–12 school system lacks accreditation, its graduates lose the opportunity to attend certain colleges or earn scholarships.

School boards are better off sustaining active accreditation status.

Procedures & Processes

As teachers, we are oh-so-familiar with the significance of procedures. I remember dedicating the first two weeks of each new school year to introducing students to the rules and procedures to which they would need to adhere in order to be successful. Similarly, there are procedures at the district level that staff must follow. Procedures are defined as a specific set of instructions for completing a single task within a process. Sometimes, procedures are inserted directly into policy. For example, in GCPS, we are drafting a new Title IX Sex Discrimination/Sexual Harassment policy in response to federal regulation changes. The new policy will incorporate procedures on how to report instances of discrimination and harassment. District leaders believe that the inclusion of procedures within the policy is essential. All stakeholders will be informed on what steps to follow to report sex discrimination and sexual harassment, whether as a personal victim or as someone made aware of the act.

Incorporating procedure into policy is typically not deemed a best practice. Imagine if every policy was inclusive of procedures. The primary drawback of such a practice is that the policy will need to be updated each time there is a change to procedure (no matter how minute the change). Consider, for example, a policy that addresses the use of school facilities. Suppose the district decides that, instead of submitting a request to the school secretary, the request now needs to be submitted to the assistant principal. This update will need to be made within the policy. In isolation, this does not appear to be a heavy lift. However, now consider the number of policies within a school district. In GCPS, we have about 170 different policies. Updating single words and phrases within a bank of policies this large requires dedicated manpower. In addition, the board will need to review the slight changes, resulting in less time to execute other board business, such as the review of student achievement data. Updating written procedures within a policy can involve extensive time and resources. For this reason, it is best to keep procedure and policy separate.

Knowing the difference between process and procedure is valuable as a board member. While a procedure is a specific set of steps or instructions that describe how to complete a task, a process focuses on achieving a defined result and includes procedures. Transitioning from the start of a project to its finish requires the implementation of processes. These processes are likely developed with the input of multiple stakeholders to arrive at an effective and efficient workflow. Organizations typically use flow charts to help illuminate parts of a process and identify who will be involved.

As a board member, you should strive to be knowledgeable of school system processes. You serve as the connector between the school district and the families being served. Oftentimes, families have questions about school processes, and they need support with understanding how to navigate the system. That is where you, as a board member, can lend expertise. You assist students and their families with getting in touch with the right people within the district who can resolve issues. Note that I did not say that you should be the one to resolve the issue. This is a key distinction that board members should keep close to their conscience. *Board members do not function to fix things in the school system.* Their role is to hold the district accountable for meeting the needs of students and families. Board members certainly provide support and establish the vision for the system, but they do not engage in operations (and operations are what drive solutions or the fixing of problems).

Board members should advance inclusivity as a cornerstone of the school district. One of the superpowers of a board member is engaging constituents and community members in school system processes as appropriate. For example, in Gwinnett, a GEMS Oversight Committee is formed annually to review new standards before formally adopting them as the curriculum to be taught in classrooms. The committee, composed of caregivers, community members, and employees of the school district, also revises standards currently implemented in the classroom. Such a practice is one of many that a school system can put in place to cultivate trust and buy-in from stakeholders. Note that there are numerous *procedures* inherent in the *process* used by the committee to review standards.

People

Now we arrive at the most important 'P' pertaining to school governance: PEOPLE. There is an old African proverb that states, "If you want to go fast, go alone; if you want to go far, go together." Improving student outcomes for ALL requires going the distance. An effective governance team understands the importance of developing a community among students, caregivers, business owners, residents, and organizations. Let's explore some of the dynamics of relationships that are imperative to advancing student achievement as a board member.

Board Member & Superintendent Relationship

Board members work with a superintendent to govern a school system. The board establishes the vision and provides input on goal-setting as to *what* the organization should seek to accomplish. The superintendent, on the other hand, directs *how* the district goes about achieving the what. A common catchphrase among school board members is, "I don't manage operations." This is imperative for stakeholders to understand because they often come to school board members expecting us to do just that. School board members generally do *not* have control of the following:

- Hiring/firing district- or school-level staff

- Modifying processes or procedures

- Changing bus routes

- Student admissions/transfers into schools

- Sporting rules, guidelines, and decisions

- Assignment of grades

- Graduation determination

- Administration of discipline consequences (excepting board involvement in the appeal process)

- Lunch choices

- Assessment calendar (the type and frequency of tests administered)

- School closures due to inclement weather and/or special events

The aforementioned are all decisions made by and managed under the direction of the school system superintendent. Board members are certainly expected to advocate on behalf of stakeholders to influence decisions made by district leadership. Board members will also be afforded the opportunity to vote to approve actions taken by the district. Note, however, that the board does not vote on ALL actions taken by the school district. The occurrence of a board vote is limited to protocol reflected in the policies of the school district. As a school board member, it is essential to help the community understand your role (determine *the what*) versus the role of the superintendent (determine and implement *the how*) when it comes to school system operations.

As you might imagine, a school system runs most productively when the superintendent cultivates a transparent relationship with board members. This is achieved through constant, two-way communication that is timely and clear. A board member should not be surprised by information published in the media or received from stakeholders in the community. Similarly, a superintendent should not be surprised by the decisions of board members or messages shared with the community by board members. Both parties are responsible for keeping the other informed ahead of the masses. The absence of doing so breeds an environment of mistrust. Without trust, the school system cripples, and a decline in student outcomes will surely follow. So, how can a culture of trust be developed and maintained? Well, I am glad you asked!

Practices to Cultivate Trust

When you think of your most valuable and treasured relationships, how would you describe them? For me personally, I think about the frequency of communication and vulnerability that exists in the exchange of messages with the other person. There is a shared understanding when it comes to the idea of confidentiality. Additionally, I trust the other person to assume goodwill and not be afraid to challenge me when appropriate. These same characteristics should be evident in a board member and superintendent relationship. Of course, such a relationship takes time to evolve, and both parties must commit to investing the time as needed.

One way to build trust is to engage in one-on-one meetings with the superintendent. This time will allow you to share your personal values and priorities with the sole individual charged with directing the activities of the school system. You also have the opportunity to learn more about what is important to the superintendent and what drives their decision making. Remember, *people don't care what you know unless they know that you care.* Both parties should take advantage of one-on-one time to expound upon why they care about student success and what their beliefs are around topics such as the significance of public education, equity, student learning, parental engagement, and community involvement, among others.

Another way to cultivate trust among governance team members (which includes all board members and the superintendent) is through shared participation in professional development. The sky's the limit for a governance team that possesses a growth mindset! I often remind my governance team that 'continuous improvement' is a high priority of mine. Even when progress is being made, you can count on me to inquire about how we might accelerate or carry over the success to other pertinent areas. Possessing a growth mindset is the cornerstone of continuous improvement. *Exerting effort to maintain the status quo (unless the current status is at the top of the charts) does not demonstrate commitment to continuous improvement.* It is, therefore, important that the governance team pursue professional learning. Gaining knowledge and a shared understanding of relevant practices and pursuits that can propel the school district's achievements can equip a team to move "far...together," as expressed in the African proverb. Shared knowledge establishes a foundation for agreeability as it pertains to goal-setting. When individuals agree on the next steps, the resulting momentum can be tremendous.

A governance team operating in agreement can indeed signal trust. Not operating in agreement, however, does not necessarily indicate mistrust. There will, rightfully and justifiably, be some issues that members of a governance team are not able to agree upon, hence the beauty of diverse thought. If everyone thought the same, creativity and innovation would be limited. Governance teams must VALUE diverse thought and not SILENCE it. Members of the team should be able to express themselves without being ignored or, even worse, retaliated against.

A final practice to foster trust among governance team members is the implementation of routine retreats. Planning for extended periods of time together in person allows for more in-depth discussions and less formal interactions. Individuals can interact more organically. A retreat offers a less structured, more relaxed meeting environment that juxtaposes the monthly work sessions and board meetings that are live-streamed and recorded. Retreats allow time for team building. Time should be dedicated to non-business activities so governance team members can learn more about each other on a personal level. With the proper planning and intentionality, retreats can significantly impact relationships across governance team members.

Board Member & District Staff Relationships

Board members should rely on the expertise of district staff to inform decision making. Staff are knowledgeable of district practices and ideally possess experience that will equip them to provide board members with precise insights. It is essential that board members be provided with accurate information since it will be shared with community members. Dispersing faulty information discredits reliability and damages relationships. Board members and district staff must therefore have and execute a relationship built on transparency and trust.

It can prove difficult for a board member to build relationships with staff if the superintendent of the district limits access to people. For example, the superintendent may specify that all queries be directed to them directly and that responses likewise be provided directly from the superintendent. If board members are not permitted to interact with district staff regularly, it will be difficult to cultivate a relationship. Board members should strive to help the superintendent see the value in allowing for more trust in the free flow of communication among key players. Board members should advocate for meetings that include district staff. For example, on my board, the superintendent sometimes invites two board members (ensuring no quorum) to meet with him and the chief of operations—or the chief of teaching and learning—to dig more deeply into organizational strategy. District leaders should also be invited to participate in governance team training or retreats to engage in team building and strategic planning discussions.

Fostering relationships with staff at the school level is invaluable for a board member. Principals and teachers are on the frontlines of teaching each day. They can best articulate the needs of learners, families, and the broader community. Board members should regularly visit schools to hear directly from core stakeholders. In my district, school councils are formed and meet quarterly to discuss goals and progress. The meetings are open to the public and typically include a leadership team inclusive of parents and business representatives. I regard school council meetings as one of the most insightful engagement opportunities a board member can attend. With regular attendance, collegial relationships develop organically, meaning staff view board members as invested partners and treat them as such, providing more detailed accounts of the realities faced in school every day. When board members are informed with the truth, they can advocate for pragmatic solutions. In the absence of learning about the authentic, lived experiences of stakeholders, board members are left in the dark as to how to direct funds and leverage policy to impact educational outcomes.

Our board has the privilege of meeting with the Teacher Advisory Council at least once each year. It is during this time that teacher representatives from across the district dialogue with board members about which initiatives and practices are effective and which might be improved. As a result of the meeting, board members are better informed on the needs of the schools and communities they serve. Resultingly, board members can advocate in a more targeted manner and approve budgetary spending aligned with expressed needs.

Board Member & Constituency or Community Member Relationships

Board members are elected to office by a constituency. A constituency is simply a body of voters who elect a representative. Gwinnett County Public Schools is made up of five districts, and I was elected to represent District IV. I am one of five board members governing the school district.

Constituency is a broad term that encompasses a vast number of subgroups, including but not limited to the following:

- Parents, guardians, and caregivers

- Students (eligible to vote)

- Local residents

- Business owners and employees

- Organizational leaders and staff

It is important to note that not everyone who identifies with the subgroups above is a constituent. Remember, a constituency is a body of voters; not all community members are eligible to vote. Nevertheless, the voices of non-eligible voters must be included in the education process. Anyone impacted by the public education of students is believed to have a stake in the school system and is therefore identified as a stakeholder whose needs should be considered, uplifted, and met as appropriate and deemed possible. There is no place for bias and preference in working to meet the needs of diverse students and families. Board members must govern in a way that welcomes collaboration, resulting in that which is best for each and every learner.

Some of the most direct ways I connect with community members is through participation in school council meetings and parent-teacher(-student) association meetings, also known as PTA or PTSA meetings. School councils are mandated in our district and exist in part to strengthen partnerships between schools and communities. The councils also function to engage parents in the decision-making process, with the ultimate goal of improving academic achievement and support for teachers and administrators. GCPS school councils meet at least four times throughout the year. Meetings are typically spent reviewing some type of data, whether it is academic, disciplinary, or some other metric indicator of student performance. Teachers and other staff provide additional context regarding student and stakeholder experiences. Parents are encouraged to chair the council and set the agenda alongside the school principal. Business partners are also invited to participate.

The level of engagement of the school council often varies from site to site. I have attended a school council with 20-30 people in attendance and a school council with fewer than ten people in attendance. What I will note about the council with the most attendees is that it was a high school council with parents and teachers from the feeder schools attending the meeting. Yes, I said teachers from the feeder schools were in attendance, and the meeting took place *DURING THE SCHOOL DAY*. This means the principals of the feeder elementary and middle schools made allowances for staff to be out of the building to attend a council meeting at the high school. While some school leaders consider it too risky or not worth the hassle of securing a substitute to allow a teacher to be absent from the classroom, this cluster of schools focused on the value added. Encouraging cluster-wide teacher participation demonstrates respect for teachers as professionals, juxtaposing the treatment of teachers as glorified babysitters. Leveraging such a teacher leadership role builds trust across staff in the cluster and supports consistent and clear communication across schools.

Similar to the school council, PTA/PTSAs cultivate an environment in which school stakeholders coalesce to solve problems. Both school council and PTA/PTSA meetings are ideal listening hubs for board members. I gather insights that empower me to be a more informed advocate and decision maker on behalf of those I serve. I remember meeting with a pastor in the community during my first campaign and explaining to him the importance of my ability to make decisions on behalf of constituents and stakeholders. His response to me was that it would be impossible to connect with each and every person in District IV due to its sheer size. He was absolutely right. It is therefore essential that I find ways to maximize engagement, both innovatively and through existing structures.

Speaking of innovation, one of the needs commonly expressed by parents and the constituency I represent is a desire to engage directly with *district* leadership. Because GCPS is so large—again, serving over 180,000 students—the district encourages families and stakeholders to connect with "school" level leaders as opposed to "district" level leaders on issues of concern. This direction encourages local control with the customization of solutions that are put in place. While the localized approach sounds astounding in theory and produces some amazing results in practice, there are times when the local school does not respond to the needs of stakeholders in a satisfactory way. In rare cases, the school offers no response at all. As a board member, this has led me to advocate for a Parent & Caregiver Advisory Council.

Interestingly enough, GCPS has a Superintendent's Student Advisory Council, a Superintendent's Business Leadership Council, and a Teacher Advisory Council. Which group of significance do you observe missing from the list? Parents and caregivers? My sentiments exactly.

Creating a structure in which caregivers have the opportunity to engage in dialogue directly with the superintendent sends a message of inclusion and value for the involvement of their voices in decision making. GCPS has a growing population of immigrant families moving into the district. Many of the parents did not attend school in the United States and are therefore uninformed on the workings of the American school system. This is but one topic worthy of discussion with a district-led Parent Advisory Council. Others include drug use, absenteeism, college and career readiness, disproportionality in discipline, and the list goes on.

I am one of two board members who use social media to frequently and consistently engage with the community. There are many advantages to developing a wide following, but there are also what some might consider disadvantages. Let me explain.

When I launched my campaign, I utilized Facebook, Instagram, and Twitter to raise awareness and share marketing materials. The ability to pay for ads targeting my electorate was valuable, and I continue to leverage Facebook and Instagram to alert stakeholders to upcoming meetings, issues impacting public education, opportunities to partner with schools or the district, and any news deserving of celebration. Besides, as a board member, you are the face of the district whether you like it or not, and the responsibility falls to you to cultivate and maintain a positive brand. While you may not consider a school to be a business, it still requires funds to run its operations. Your brand influences the level of funding that streams into the school system. Losing accreditation can be extremely damaging and detrimental to a school system. As a board member, you therefore want to elevate the high-quality achievements of your district. Doing so reassures families that they are raising their children in the right place. When families choose to live in your district, it results in federal, state, and local tax dollars being made available to educate students. Now, whether or not the amount of funding made available is adequate... That is another book topic in and of itself. For now, let us stick to the importance of asserting a positive brand as a way to retain stakeholder trust and commitment.

Another insightful way I leverage social media is to explain the 'why' behind my votes. As board members, we are charged with voting to approve numerous actions across the school system, from the adoption of the curriculum to the approval of staff hiring and the implementation of new policies. While many actions we vote on are of little consequence or interest, particularly when approving the action results in business as usual, there are times when a vote may be deemed controversial. For example, our board was presented with a sexual education curriculum for adoption last year. The curriculum being proposed for adoption was a shift from our traditional approach to sex education, which encouraged abstinence. The new curriculum instead focused on how to engage in safe practices should you choose to have sex. Ultimately, the consensus of the board was to forgo adopting the new resource and instead repeat the adoption process, fostering full transparency along the way. The process used in this cycle was no different from the process used in previous cycles of curriculum adoption. There was no reason to believe or evidence to support that the district was not transparent as it pertains to the process this resource underwent. However, because a number of constituents were vocal about their disappointment with the results of the process, the board consented to start the process again.

In times of controversy, social media can help to elevate your personal motivations around a vote. You can inform stakeholders on how you voted and why. While it is important to support board decisions in public—because, as I said before, a school system is a business that requires positive branding—it is just as important for people to know why your personal vote did or did not align with the consensus. Governance entails disagreement, and governance team members should cultivate an environment of being okay with that disagreement. If everyone on a governance team agreed with each other all the time, that would be cause for concern.

The last strategy I would like to highlight as a best practice in connecting with school stakeholders is perhaps the most 'old school' communication practice that exists today other than letter writing—pick up the phone and make a call. It is arguably the simplest and most effective way to build relationships. There is something to be said about hearing someone's voice on the other side of the issue. The passion is perhaps less evasive, while tone and mood are more vivid when engaged in dialogue as opposed to typing or texting back and forth. Of course, meeting in person adds an extra layer of context, allowing for responses to visual cues. However, if striving to maintain a work-life balance is a priority, making phone calls will likely be more easily achievable than meeting with people face-to-face. As a tip, be sure to let stakeholders know at the beginning of the call how much time you have available to speak. Sharing the length of your availability manages expectations around how much information can or should be shared now as opposed to later. It also prevents the stakeholder from being caught off guard, should you need to interrupt to end the call or reschedule a follow-up phone call.

Board Member & Student Relationships

I would submit that no school board member would object to enhancing the quantity and quality of interactions they have with students. GCPS instituted a Superintendent's Student Advisory Council in 2022, providing an avenue for students in grades 6-12 to engage directly with the superintendent on issues affecting them, their schools, and their communities. Because the school board is responsible for creating and approving district-wide policies that address concerns, it would benefit the school board to engage with a student council as well. An opportunity exists for a similar structure to be launched in support of feedback exchanges between board members and students.

Across the nation, there is a rise in the number of school boards striving to include the student voice as a member of the governance team. While in many cases the student is not afforded voting rights, the student is granted agency to share experiences and provide feedback that will inform and hopefully influence those who are permitted to vote.

Board members can certainly leverage grassroots efforts to connect with students throughout the community. One of my fellow board members created a structure of her own accord and now meets with students throughout the year. Partnering with the Parent-Teacher-Student Association is another way board members can gather insights from students to influence decision making.

One of the fundamental purposes of public education is to prepare students for a life that includes civic responsibility. When students graduate, they enter society as contributing adults. It only makes sense that we invite them into the school system governance process so that we better understand their needs. A school board has the authority to funnel dollars and create policies that can greatly alter the experiences of learners within a school system. With intimate knowledge of the needs and wants of students, boards are more adequately equipped to do what is best with the knowledge that these same students will someday be leading our communities and the country at large.

Taking on the role of a school board member is a huge commitment. You can positively impact the trajectory of not just one student's life but hundreds or even thousands of students' lives. As an educator, you know the ins and outs of the job. You have a front-row seat to how policy looks in practice. You implement districtwide procedures and processes on a day-to-day basis within your school. You know the people, the stakeholders, because you interact with them constantly within your community. Why not use all of that wisdom and experience to wield power in the best interests of students? Do not willingly hand over that power to someone who lacks the intricate insight you bring to the table. You know what it takes to propel student achievement. Your school board needs you!

Teacher Takeover Testimonial

When I first moved to Georgia from Nevada, I had the pleasure of meeting Adrienne Simmons. At that time, I was struggling to adjust to the educational environment in the Atlanta metro area. Adrienne's unwavering positivity and insightful suggestions were incredibly encouraging. She motivated me to explore different school districts and persist in my career in education.

Years later, Dr. Simmons took on the role of an elected school board member for Gwinnett County Schools, where she has truly exemplified what it means to wear many hats. Her dedication is evident in her constant presence and active involvement in the community. Whether attending school functions or advocating for change, she manages to balance her responsibilities with grace while fulfilling her roles as a wife and working mother. Her remarkable commitment to both schools and the community continues to inspire me and has greatly influenced my own path toward leadership. I am currently a Computer Science Specials Teacher and First Lego League Coach with the goal of getting my Educational Specialist in Instructional Technology.

Virginia Watkins
Computer Science Teacher

CHAPTER 7

The Significance of Self-Care and How to Achieve Work-Life Balance

I can vividly remember feeling completely dreadful while driving to work during my last year of teaching before becoming an instructional coach. My anxiety was through the roof. I was teaching third grade, which was a new grade level for me. I had previously taught first grade for four years. A significant number of my third graders were not reading on grade level, although I cannot say this was unexpected. I knew the academic standing of my school very well, having served as schoolwide design team co-chair for two years. But it was not just the academic challenges that were weighing me down. I was having a tough time getting my students' parents engaged, and behavior issues were a constant distraction from the learning. For additional context, I was experiencing this feeling of being overwhelmed pre-COVID pandemic, when not as many people were concerned with the well-being of teachers. I knew my mental health was in jeopardy...I was in desperate need of a break.

This scenario is way too common and applies to educators across the country. We keep going and going and going like the Energizer Bunny, oftentimes until the battery dies. Many of us strive for perfection in the classroom at the expense of our health. As educators, we have to change our mindset. Perfection should not be our aspiration; nobody is perfect. What you don't get done today can be done tomorrow. Now, I'm certainly not condoning slothfulness. Our students deserve to be taught by professionals who show up prepared and motivated to mold lives. As a matter of fact, our marginalized students *must* have educators who show up ready to overcome challenges. On the contrary, what I am condoning is permission to take a breather. Permit yourself to incorporate mindfulness activities into your own routine and that of your students, and permit yourself to take time off from work to tend to your physical and emotional well-being. Miss a deadline or two...without making it a habit, of course. Do not beat yourself up for being human. Do not set expectations so high that attaining them is unrealistic or detrimental to your health. Instead, embrace the idea of being a perfectly imperfect professional in pursuit of success for all learners.

Begin documenting and reflecting on your self-care practices using the Mental Health Tracker at www.TeacherTakeover.com/toolkit.

The Power of Sick Days and Employee Assistance Programs

One of the most profound pieces of advice I received as an early educator is that using sick days is not just for times when you are physically ill; maintaining your mental wholeness is just as important. Think about when you are aboard a plane, and the flight attendant tells you to put on your oxygen mask before attempting to help anyone else. The same rule applies in the classroom. Your physical and mental health come first. For some, the act of prioritizing oneself feels selfish, but it is okay to be selfish when it comes to caring for your body, mind, and spirit. Teaching requires an extensive amount of pouring out; you pour out into the minds of numerous children on a daily basis. You cannot give something you do not have. In order to pour out, you have to be full—and continuously refilled. There should be no shame in utilizing your sick days to rest and reset. Students are more likely to reach their full potential when you show up as your best self.

In addition to sick days, there are additional benefits that organizations typically offer through Employee Assistance Programs. In Gwinnett County Public Schools, all benefit-eligible employees, including retirees, are offered behavioral health and counseling services at no charge. The offering aligns with the district's strategic plan of promoting staff well-being through the prioritization of physical health, mental health, and self-care. The service is delivered by an authorized healthcare provider and serves to help employees with stress management. Licensed counselors are available to support staff dealing with issues such as divorce, financial hardship, and various other significant life changes.

I recently took advantage of counseling services while experiencing grief due to the loss of a loved one. I was offered five sessions free of charge and benefited tremendously. In addition, I used sick hours to attend to my mental health in the days and weeks following the tragic loss (since it wasn't an immediate family member who passed away, I could not use bereavement leave). Needless to say, sick hours should be used for mental health just as readily as they are used for physical health. In the absence of mental wholeness, productivity suffers. In the case of education, when teachers are not mentally whole, student learning is negatively impacted.

Get Moving

In my twenties, when I first started teaching, I did not feel the need to work out. I was pretty slim up until that point and did not have to do much to maintain my "girlish figure." What I came to realize later in life, however, is that exercise is not just for weight loss. It actually serves as a stress reliever and can help to build a sense of camaraderie with others working out alongside you. Despite the unappealing rap it might get, exercise helps to improve mental wellness. The enhancement of your physique is, of course, an added benefit.

When I finally started working out, I struggled with consistency. I would go to L.A. Fitness once or twice a week and leave 30 minutes after I arrived. My routine consisted of walking or running on the treadmill and grabbing a few sips of water. Sometimes, I would take a group class instead that required me to do grapevines and other fun moves in sync with the directions of the instructor. One day reality hit me -- the only way I was going to become more disciplined in my workout routine is if I had an instructor to tell me exactly what to do for the entirety of my time in the gym. I can't be trusted to work out on my own...I'm just being honest. I now have a membership at a gym that provides group training, inclusive of weightlifting and cardio workouts. It's been about three years since I first joined the gym, and even my husband has been surprised at my consistency.

Seeing physical changes in my body has encouraged me to continue exercising. I feel ready to take on the day after a good workout, with more mental alertness and a sense of accomplishment. Contrary to belief, I am not tired after exercising. Instead, I feel as though I've gained a couple of extra hours in the day because I am so pumped up and energized. I will admit it took some time to achieve this state of being, but after about a month or two, working out became a part of my lifestyle.

During the spring and fall (and sometimes winter here in Georgia), I complement my gym workouts with a visit to the neighborhood trail for an outdoor walk, run, or bike ride. Yes...during the pandemic, my family was one of the many that invested in bikes! And thank goodness we did. We have explored so much of the community and surrounding cities that we never ventured to visit before, all while burning calories and enhancing our mental health.

Find Momentum in Mentorship

"Work smarter, not harder." Those were the words of one of my most profound mentors, who we'll call Charity. Charity showed up in my life as a co-worker during my first year of teaching. She taught first grade in the room directly next to mine. At the time, our school was undergoing renovation, so we were temporarily housed in an older school building that was no longer utilized full-time by the school district. We did not have the pleasure of teaching in a room closed off by four walls and a door. Instead, our classrooms were connected to one another by a door frame with no door attached. As a result, I heard nearly everything that was said in her class and vice versa. Imagine the difficulty of teaching a lesson and not being able to close off any distracting noises from other students and staff members engaged in learning activities. It sure wasn't easy, but we made it work. Anyhow, Charity taught me so much in my early years as an educator—and not just in words but in action.

As a first-year teacher, I was amazed by Charity's ability to show up to work, teach effectively, and leave *on time* every day. I emphasize the words "on time" because, as educators, we know that working late almost appears to be a requirement despite not getting paid overtime. Charity seemed to possess some type of magic, and I honestly wanted to learn her tricks. Over time, she helped me to adopt and enact the "work smarter, not harder" mentality, which has become a lifesaver.

So, what exactly does it mean to work smarter and not harder? In the most basic form, it entails maximizing productivity while minimizing inputs of time and energy. Putting the mantra into practice will look different for each individual. In my life, it has shown up consistently as establishing routines and systems to minimize my investment of time. For example, instead of making paper copies for one lesson at a time, I began making copies for a week of lessons at a time. This 'smarter' way of planning helped to cut down on my return visits to the copy room, allowing more time for the completion of other tasks during the regularly scheduled workday. I also began leveraging classroom helpers to minimize my input of energy, which simultaneously helped develop leadership skills in my young learners. Students excelled in taking care of our classroom plants, reviewing assignments, organizing the classroom library by genre, etc. They not only learned responsibility but took on a greater sense of pride in their classroom and classwork.

'Integrating the curriculum' was a hot buzz phrase during my early years of teaching. Whether intentional or not, it cultivated a "work harder, not smarter" approach as it pertains to my personal pedagogy. I remember creating a behavior system that allowed students to earn "money" throughout the week that would be cashed in for positive incentives on Friday. The system required students to learn how to count money (which was a grade-level academic standard) and manage a ledger, which I am sure you would agree is an invaluable life tool. The system was so innovative that it prompted my principal to invite administrators from outside the state to visit my classroom. Working smarter and not harder paid off in countless ways.

One of the reasons I admired Charity so much was because, at a time when I appeared to struggle with time management as a single woman with no children of my own, she made teaching look flawless as a married mother of two. Over time, I came to learn that looks can be deceiving; she, like me, had struggles to overcome in finding a work-life balance. However, her students appeared to always be engaged in the learning process and were consistently meeting high expectations. These were the markings of a phenomenal teacher in my novice eyes. Through getting to know Charity better, I became knowledgeable of her more personal routines, such as eating healthily, running regularly, attending church weekly, and going out to dance occasionally. She engaged in several outlets to prevent her professional life from becoming overwhelming, and she not only kept her kids busy in extracurricular activities but actively participated in their swim meets to cheer them on. Through both words and actions, Charity taught me how to become a well-rounded educator capable of showing up whole, both in the classroom and out.

I was lucky to connect with someone like Charity early on in my career. Nowadays, many school systems employ formal mentorship programs in which they pair up novice teachers with more experienced educators. Take full advantage of this opportunity by being vulnerable and willing to learn. Working in public education can be tough. Add to that navigating unspoken rules in your school, and quitting begins to appear more and more appealing. Mentorship can provide a lifeline and may very well be the reason you not only survive but thrive as a teacher.

Prioritize Fun

Achieving a work-life balance is no easy feat. As educators, we often neglect ourselves in the spirit of serving. We serve our students, their families, our administrators, co-workers, and others within the organization. We then go home to serve our own families with what energy and reserves we have left. This is a cycle of destruction. It is also a form of self-neglect.

I recently came across an article explaining the definition of 'decision fatigue' and how it applies to the lives of educators. In a nutshell, educators make an extraordinary number of decisions each day as a result of being responsible for the actions and well-being of 20+ students. The requirement to make scores of decisions day in and day out takes a mental toll on a person. Fatigue sets in. Teachers owe it to themselves to discover outlets that minimize the necessity to make countless decisions. Just this month, I celebrated my birthday with a group of friends and made it known that "I don't want to make any decisions." That particular weekend of not having the responsibility of making plans for other people left me satisfactorily reinvigorated.

My younger sister often compliments my ability to prioritize fun. As a married mother of two working a full-time job while also governing on the school board, I could easily become consumed with the responsibilities of life. However, I have learned to say "no" to invitations and expectations of others when it is in my best interests. Similarly, I have learned to say "yes" to self-care and fun. Whether it is a vacation somewhere tropical with my husband, a cabin trip with girlfriends, or a Beyoncé concert with my sisters, I find the time to unwind and recharge. There are only so many hours in a day. If I said "yes" to every opportunity presented in my endeavor to impact the lives of learners and their families, I would not have time for my own family, friends, and other personal ambitions. Setting boundaries is essential to accomplishing and sustaining a work-life balance.

What setting boundaries looks like for me is blocking out time on my work calendar for lunch and breaks every day. I manage my calendar in a way that allows for routine workouts and even therapy sessions when needed. Yes, I said therapy. Aside from dealing with grief from the loss of life, I've dealt with and will continue to deal with issues stemming simply from living life. A good therapist can make the road to recovery more swift, attainable, and enduring. I believe in the power of prayer as well as professional support. Do not be afraid to reach out to a therapist or even multiple therapists if needed. In my case, the first therapist I worked with was unprofessional, showing up to calls late and eating during our sessions. However, the second time around was much more fulfilling. I was paired with someone who was a great listener, easy to talk to, and extremely resourceful. As a result, I now possess an enhanced mindset and helpful tools to combat inevitable future situations that will arise along this journey called life.

Having fun should not be an afterthought. You must be intentional about making plans to spend time with family and friends. You should engage in activities you enjoy on a routine basis, whether they be dancing, listening to music, going to the theatre, sewing, traveling, etc. Making plans outside of work cultivates a healthy balance, which is especially necessary when working in demanding conditions. Moving a student by more than one grade level within a year, which has been made even more necessary as a result of COVID-induced learning loss, can cause mental exhaustion. In addition to planning for differentiated instruction, resources must be secured and prepared before execution can even occur. Next comes the evaluation, and then the cycle repeats itself: plan, prepare, execute, evaluate. A myriad of complexities exist in each segment of the cycle, but this is not news to you. Ultimately, you need to give yourself permission to step outside of the cycle. The cycle can't come home with you every day; the cycle must be vacated daily. Do not commit all of your waking hours to working! It is not healthy. Your mental and physical health will not be sustained. Find joy outside of work and boldly pursue intriguing experiences and new adventures. Your mind, body, and soul will thank you.

Teacher Takeover Testimonial

I met Adrienne Simmons during my first year as a teacher, when she served as my instructional coach. From the beginning, Adrienne's kindness and unwavering support made a profound impact on me. She approached every challenge with a calm demeanor and a genuine commitment to helping others succeed.

I have been able to truly witness Adrienne's remarkable qualities—her relentless work ethic, her dedication to her craft, and her inspiring ability to balance work and life. She not only encouraged me to pursue leadership opportunities but also motivated me to further my education. Adrienne's guidance was instrumental in shaping my approach to both my professional and personal development.

The principles and practices I observed in Adrienne have been invaluable to me. Her strategic approach to career advancement, coupled with her commitment to maintaining a harmonious work-life balance, provided me with essential insights. Applying these lessons has been pivotal in my own journey, allowing me to advance to the role of Area Coordinator in Georgia's third-largest school district.

Adrienne Simmons exemplifies the qualities of an exceptional mentor and leader. Her influence has left an indelible mark on my career, and I am deeply grateful for the opportunity to have worked with her and to consider her a friend.

Tiffany Townsend

Area Coordinator

CHAPTER 8

Ready...Set...Act!

———

It is my hope that this book has motivated you to continue in your pursuit of making a difference in the lives of children. You have been equipped with several strategies to advocate, lead, and govern while prioritizing your mental health. Now, you must act.

Within the next week, I challenge you to take the first step. Consider the following:

- Reach out to a parent to tell them how much you enjoy having their child in your class. Remember, this establishes a relationship that cultivates authority in your classroom.

- Collaborate with fellow teachers to implement a solution addressing a need within the school.

- Comment at a school board meeting to inform leaders on challenges facing students and their families.

- Take a walk in the park, seek a mentor, or attend a comedy show to reclaim your mental health.

- Begin planning your campaign to run for the school board.

It doesn't matter WHERE you start; what is important is that you DO start. Oftentimes, the most difficult step is the first one. I'm reminded of when my daughter started walking for the very first time. The first couple of steps were wobbly and unstable. However, after a while, she caught on and quickly progressed from walking to running. That will be your experience along *The Teacher Takeover* journey. Initially, you may experience some discomfort. You may even fall or experience what appears to be failure. If this happens, choose to fail forward. Every experience teaches a lesson. Reflect on what happened, how you responded, what you could have done differently (if anything), and how you will grow from the situation. Access the Fail Forward Framework at www.TeacherTakeover.com/toolkit to reflect on your experiences and initiate an action plan.

You can never triumph unless you try. Think about your favorite singer or actress. Many of those who have risen to fame will tell you that they had to overcome doubt and obstacles along the way. Your journey in the transformational education space will not be any different. There will be naysayers, and there will be barriers. You will get frustrated. You will experience moments of exhaustion. However, you have to commit and keep your eyes on the big picture: successful students, healthy families, and thriving communities.

Do not overthink your next move. If you are anything like me, you feel the need to plan everything out. You like to anticipate challenges so you can be prepared. Believe me...I get it! But not every teacher takeover initiative requires a well-thought-out plan. You can just go for it in some instances, and you *should* just go for it, particularly as it pertains to your mental health. Review *The Teacher Takeover* strategies to follow and decide where you will begin within the next seven days.

The Teacher Takeover ABCs

1. Advance the Teaching Profession as Deserving of More Respect

2. Advocate for Higher Salaries

3. Advocate for More Affordable or Supplementary Housing

4. Advocate for Meaningful, Timely, Ongoing Professional Development

5. Advocate for Teacher Autonomy and Speak Out Against Legislation That Impedes It

6. Acquire a Mentor

7. Abandon Perfectionism

8. Always Speak *YOUR* Truth

9. Be Student Focused

10. Be the Expert

11. Be Persistent

12. Be the Voice for Those Intentionally Silenced

13. Be Flexible in Your Leadership Style

14. Be an Activist/Community Organizer

15. Become a Legislator

16. Become a School Board Member

17. Balance Work and Life

18. Benefit from Work Benefits

19. Commit

20. Consider Transforming Educational Outcomes Your Duty

21. Connect with (and Stay Connected to) Supportive Individuals

22. Create Boundaries

23. Cast Away Imposter Syndrome

24. Cultivate Trust While Developing Relationships

25. Compel Others to Act

Download the complete list of The Teacher Takeover ABCs by visiting www.TeacherTakeover.com/toolkit.

Teacher Takeover Testimonial

Working with Dr. Adrienne Simmons has been nothing short of transformative for my business. As an emerging entrepreneur, I faced challenges in expanding my network and reaching new stakeholders and customers. Dr. Simmons provided me with strategic insights and actionable advice that opened doors I never thought possible. Her expertise in stakeholder engagement and customer acquisition was instrumental in helping me grow my education consulting business and connect with the right people. Thanks to her guidance, I've been able to build meaningful relationships that have significantly boosted my brand's visibility and impact. Dr. Simmons' support has been a game-changer for my entrepreneurial journey, and I highly recommend her to anyone looking to elevate their business to the next level.

Bejanae Kareem

BK International Education Consultancy, Founder

CHAPTER 9

Epilogue

N ow that you have read this book, you are empowered to begin reclaiming authority in your classroom, school, and personal life. You furthermore have the capacity to transform educational outcomes for students. Your life, as well as the lives of your students and their families, will be forever changed for the better.

Do not delay in implementing the strategies you have learned. Start today. Take one step at a time. Identify where you would like to begin, and put one foot in front of the other. There is no ONE way to reclaim authority, but I urge you to start immediately. Your mental health is at stake. The trajectory of student lives can be propelled forward, and communities can be completely transformed. The world is waiting for you to show up and leave an indelible mark on the lives of learners as only you can.

To follow is a summary of the key concepts presented throughout the book that serve to equip you as a leader within your school and community while prioritizing personal wellness.

Chapter 1 - Mass Exodus: This chapter explores reasons educators are leaving the profession and suggests solutions that will entice teachers to stay.

Chapter 2 - Define Your Why and Commit to the Heart Work: Reconnect to why you wanted to become a teacher in the first place. Understand that students need transformative educators like you to help meet their needs both inside and outside the classroom.

Chapter 3 – Dare to Disrupt the Status Quo: This chapter provides an overview of three distinct pathways to impactfully lead in public education. Gain insights into the concepts of traditional leadership, advocacy, and governance, which comprise the TAG framework, and how the three pathways intersect.

Chapter 4 - Traditional Leadership: Discover school leadership styles essential to impacting the lives of marginalized communities. Work through scenarios to practice adapting your leadership style to enhance staff morale, cultivate inclusivity, manage student behavior, and better engage caregivers.

Chapter 5 - Advocacy: Unpack advocate-worthy causes in the field of education and gain insights into how to advocate effectively for students and their families to enhance academic outcomes.

Chapter 6 - Governance: Understand the role and responsibilities of a board member in governing a school system. Discover best practices through exploration of the 5P Framework for School Board Governance.

Chapter 7 - The Significance of Self-Care and How to Achieve Work-Life Balance: Gain clarity on how to prioritize personal health while sustaining influence on the job. Understand the health benefits afforded to teachers and ways to offset the pressures that come with working in public education.

Chapter 8 - Ready...Set...Act!: Now is the time to apply what you have learned. Some actions will require planning, but others will not. Don't think your way out of making progress.

The students sitting in your classroom are our future leaders. What they accomplish tomorrow depends in part on the actions you take today. There is no time to waste. Doing school as usual is no longer an option if it does not serve you, your students, and their families. Step into your power as a transformational educator and take over!

NOTES

INTRODUCTION

11 **Figure 1. TAG Framework**: Simmons, A. (2024). Created using Canva. (https://www.canva.com/).

CHAPTER 1. MASS EXODUS

16 **This is a place where the typical value of a home**: https://www.zillow.com/home-values/37211/atlanta-ga/.

18 **Katie Rinderlie, a 10-year veteran teacher**: Gaunt, R. (2023). https://cobbcountycourier.com/2023/06/interview-with-cobb-teacher-fired-over-book-under-georgias-divisive-concepts-law/.

18 **The city of Atlanta, just 15 minutes down the road**: Human Rights Campaign Foundation. https://hrc-prod-requests.s3-us-west-2.amazonaws.com/MEI-2022-Atlanta-Georgia.pdf.

20 **Some indicators used to measure the overall respect of teachers**: Walker, T. (2018). https://www.nea.org/nea-today/all-news-articles/where-do-teachers-get-most-respect.

CHAPTER 2. DEFINE YOUR WHY AND COMMIT TO THE HEART WORK

25 **A social media post communicating**: Settles, G. (2022). https://www.politifact.com/factchecks/2022/jul/20/instagram-posts/no-third-grade-reading-scores-are-not-being-used-p/.

26 **New data from the U.S. Census reveals**: Shrider, E. and Creamer, J. (2023). https://www.census.gov/library/publications/2023/demo/p60-280.html#:~:text=The%20SPM%20child%20poverty%20rate,peopl e%20out%20of%20SPM%20poverty.

CHAPTER 3. DARE TO DISRUPT THE STATUS QUO

36 **Figure 2. Pathways to Disrupting the Status Quo**: Simmons, A. (2024). AI-Generated Content. https://designer.microsoft.com/image-creator.

CHAPTER 5. ADVOCATE

61 **Maslow posits that our needs are what motivate us**: Maslow, A.H. (1943). A Theory of Human Motivation. Psychological Review, 50, 370-396. http://dx.doi.org/10.1037/h0054346.

62 **Figure 3. Maslow's Hierarchy of Needs**: Androidmarsexpress, CC BY-SA 4.0. https://creativecommons.org/licenses/by-sa/4.0, via Wikimedia Commons.

68 **Schools should commit to addressing**: ASCD Whole Child. https://library.ascd.org/m/1f2720c1c2296a94/original/ASCD-Whole-Child-Action-Plan-Guide.pdf.

72 **I'm reminded of the biblical character Moses**: Exodus 4:10.

CHAPTER 6. GOVERNANCE

83 **In fact, Georgia state law dictates**:
https://law.justia.com/codes/georgia/2010/title-20/chapter-2/article-3/20-2-49/.

www.ingramcontent.com/pod-product-compliance
Lightning Source LLC
Chambersburg PA
CBHW061652120626
46550CB00003B/916